# The
# Sociology of
# Modernization
# and Development

# The Sociology of Modernization and Development

**DAVID HARRISON**

*University of Sussex*

London and New York

First published 1988 by Unwin Hyman Ltd
Second impression 1990

Reprinted 1991 and 1993
by Routledge
11 New Fetter Lane, London EC4P 4EE

Simultaneously published in the USA and Canada
by Routledge
29 West 35th Street, New York, NY 10001

Printed and bound in Great Britain by
Biddles Ltd, Guildford and King's Lynn

*British Library Cataloguing in Publication Data*

Harrison, David, *1941 –*
    The sociology of modernization and development.
    1. Developing countries. Modernization Sociolopolitical aspects.
    I. Title.
    909'.097240828

*Library of Congress Cataloging in Publication Data*

Harrison, David, 1941 –
    The sociology of modernization and development.
    Bibliography: p.
    Includes index.
    1. Economic development – Social aspects. I. Title
    HD75.H35   1988   306'.3       88-5631

ISBN 0-415-07870-9

*In memory of*
*Valerie Awang and Selwyn Mendoza*

# Contents

# Preface

In the early 1970s, when I first carried out empirical research in the Caribbean, I spent almost a year and a half in a small Caribbean village. It had around 500 inhabitants, 50 per cent of whom were under the age of 15, and its history had been dominated by the rise and fall of the cocoa industry of Trinidad, an industry which owed much of its success to the collective sweet tooth of generations of British children and the demand of British chocolate manufacturers for Trinidadian cocoa. When children's tastes changed, or when there were improvements in cocoa refining techniques, the villagers were crucially, sometimes cruelly, affected.

The villagers had also been influenced by the increased prosperity of a young Scot who, so the story goes, went to Trinidad in the 1860s with a few pounds in his pocket, and became one of the leading landowners and politicians in Trinidad. Many years later, his son was sent to Eton and was to become (when he left the Caribbean) one of the richest landowners in Scotland. Much of this wealth came from Trinidad, not just from the village and not just from cocoa, but his fortune was undoubtedly founded in the cocoa industry, and in land acquired, one way or another, from countless Trinidadian peasants.

By Western standards, the villagers were poor, and they were fully aware of their poverty. They lived 'behind God's back'. They wanted to do better and, if they were not young, they wanted their children or their grandchildren to better themselves: to be educated at grammar schools, to become teachers or nurses or, failing this, clerks or taxi drivers. Young people wanted and were encouraged to move to town to increase their prospects, not only to improve their chances of employment but also to be able to afford the items ready cash could buy: radios, tape-recorders and evenings at the cinema. And they did move, so much so that few of them were actually resident in the village by the time they were 20, returning only for the occasional week-end and at holiday times. The older people were left to carry on as best they could, farming their inaccessible land or persuading someone else to do it for them, and the few young people who remained attempted to safeguard their future by working for the local authority and on the state-sponsored road programme. As far as possible they avoided agriculture, which was relatively poorly paid.

At the time I wrote up my research, (Harrison, 1975) under-development theory had made little impact in departments of anthropology, but in many respects it was quite clear that the village was 'dependent' on the outside world – that is, the rest of Trinidad as well as other parts of the world system. However, although they were not as prosperous as they had been in the past, the villagers had a thriving culture which was far from a reflection of some metropolitan centre. Socialization into village life gave actors a well-understood 'life plan' of how they were expected to behave towards members of the opposite sex and towards their elders, age mates and outsiders, and the gossip network of 'Demsay' was active enough to publicize the activities of those who stepped out of line. This was not unusual: there were frequent disputes between men and women, between young and old, and between women born in the village and women born elsewhere. As one would expect, the beliefs of these descendants of Venezuelan peons and African slaves exhibited elements from Latin America, Africa and Europe. Nevertheless, their culture was their own. Although undoubtedly shaped by the experiences of their ancestors and honed by economic uncertainty, it was a vital and continuing guide to being human in Demsay. In so far as the village way of life was an 'articulation' of different traditions, modes of production, and so on, it had been brought into existence, maintained, altered and passed on by the actors themselves.

Some time after I left the village, it was provided with electricity. Most people would agree that this was a good thing. Having obtained electric light, the villagers went on to acquire television sets, and the enterprising rum shop proprietor installed a juke box. Observers of village life might have mixed feelings about such additions, but the villagers themselves were in no doubt that they were desirable.

My first 'professional' experience of the Third World was an an anthropologist, and I now find the distinction between social anthropology and sociology quite artificial. Ultimately, the sociology of modernization and development is about people, in the Third World and elsewhere, who have their own ideas of progress, who live in a socio-economic environment which they cannot fully control, and who yet have their own cultures, their charters for living. The external and the internal are both important, and the actors' views of their position should not be discounted by some fancy theorist who feels he or she knows better. At the same time, most sociologists would probably claim that their disciplined, theoretically-informed way of perceiving the social world can provide insights not immediately available to Trinidian villagers or anyone else they might have studied. Provided it is carried out with caution, scepticism and a degree of humility, the sociological attempt to understand what is happening in the social world seems to be based on a worthy aim.

The juke box and the television sets were small examples of modernization, and may or may not be considered as evidence of development. In the final chapter, I define modernization as what is 'up to date' in a specific location at any given time. It is usually the result of a process of 'Westernization', involving economic, political, social and cultural changes which contrast with a previous 'traditional' stability. Indeed, any reference to modernity seems to imply some kind of contrast with a pre-existing order, and in such circumstances conflict may occur. But other outcomes are also possible, and all that can be said with certainty is that the present is always the result of an active accommodation to, or confrontation with, the past.

Development is defined as much the same as modernization: a far-reaching, continuous, and positively evaluated change in the totality of human experience. The difference between the two concepts is that whilst there need be no argument about modernization, about what is actually happening, there will inevitably be strong disagreements as to whether or not development is also occurring. Development, then, is always a valued state, which may or may not have been achieved in some other social context, and which may not even be achievable.

In the past, modernization theorists tended to equate modernization and development. They focused largely (but not entirely) on the 'new' nation states, and assumed that what had occurred in the West could be repeated, albeit with a little help in the way of capital, technology, expertise and 'rationality'. Underdevelopment theorists and other critics of modernization theory have taken a more hostile attitude to Westernization, arguing that the expansion of Western capitalism incorporated the Third World into an exploitative world system, thus leading to its underdevelopment. They concentrated on the (mainly detrimental) links of Third World with the world system, and until recently have paid relatively little attention to the domestic structures of Third World societies.

These perspectives are partial and do not necessarily contradict one another. It is therefore mistaken to regard them as competing paradigms. As far as empirical evidence is concerned, there is a 'limited commensurability' which is clearly indicated in the ongoing debates over modernization and development in the Third World. The polemics and acrimony arise not from an analysis of empirical evidence but over the way it should be interpreted – that is, over whether or not what is happening should be regarded as 'development'. And criteria for development are not laid down by sociological theory but by ideologies, which are the subject of as much disagreement among social scientists as among other members of society. In fact, even ideologies may be modified when confronted with empirical data. As a result, some theorists are reassessing the view that capitalism is 'in crisis' and that socialism, in the Third World or elsewhere, is inevitably 'progressive'. This debate will continue and is likely to gain momentum. As I was putting the finishing touches to this book, a recent collection of articles on capitalism in the Third World was published (Berger, 1987b). Admirably illustrating the trend I have just described, it subjects the claim that capitalism leads to inequality in the Third World to empirical scrutiny. The evidence put forward is far from conclusive, but Berger suggests it favours 'the proposition that capitalist development generates powerful equalizing forces, and that it tends to do so more reliably and more humanely than its empirically socialist or statist

competitors' (1987b, p. 15). Some will reject this conclusion for
ideological reasons alone but others will take up the challenge,
and the outcome will be a renewed commitment to study the
nature of capitalism in the Third World. Provided the debate is
conducted with a degree of sociological scepticism and a due
concern for empirical accuracy, theorists of all persuasions will be
involved. They need not be convinced of the virtues of capitalism;
indeed, unbelievers may gleefully note that in Britain publication
of Berger's book more or less coincided with a collapse of the
world's financial markets. This merely emphasizes the danger of
nailing sociological colours to ideological masts.

Modernization or underdevelopment? We can argue about the
evaluations and debate the empirical evidence, but the sociology
of modernization and development embodies the concerns of
competing perspectives. We need to focus on the actor and the
system, on culture, values and political and economic change,
on diffusion and innovation, and on the importance of domestic
structures as well as links with external institutions and the
world system. As part of this study, we need also to examine the
role of social scientists themselves as active diffusers of Western
perceptions of development, be they capitalist or socialist, and to
recognize that, as it now stands, the sociology of modernization
and development is firmly located in Western intellectual traditions which go back (at least) to Marx, Durkheim and Weber.

The customary thanks will be few but genuine. I did my own
typing, so at least I have one cause for self-congratulation. Bill
Williams provided the initial challenge to write the book, and then
another along the way. Marc Williams and Sheila Smith, colleagues at
the School of African and Asian Studies, and Steven Yearley and Aidan
Foster-Carter all read sizeable sections of the manuscript. Their
comments were greatly appreciated, even if they were sometimes
(wrongly?) ignored. Greta Bowman gave me consistent support,
and Asha and Ian, our children, constantly made me aware that
there is more to life than writing books. Gordon Smith, of Unwin
Hyman, was more quietly concerned with such matters, and I
must record my gratitude for his patience and assistance. A special
word of thanks to Pete Saunders, my friend and colleague at Sussex.
He read and commented extensively on an earlier draft and was
made to discuss it, inter alia, over many a Sunday pint. I am glad
he is around in 'the lecture rooms of the university'.

Obviously, no one I have mentioned can possibly be blamed for the many errors of fact, omission, and interpretation in the following pages. The project grew more daunting every day, and I am aware that I have taken numerous hostages to fortune. It is with some trepidation that I have to accept (to give another example of diffusion) that 'the buck stops here'.

# 1

# Early Modernization Theory

## Introduction

There is no one modernization theory. Rather, this term is shorthand for a variety of perspectives that were applied by non-Marxists to the Third World in the 1950s and 1960s. The dominant themes of such perspectives arose from established sociological traditions and involved the reinterpretation, often conscious, of the concerns of classical sociology. Evolutionism (with its focus on increasing differentiation), diffusionism, structural functionalism, systems theory and interactionism all combined to help form the mish-mash of ideas that came to be known as modernization theory. There were inputs from other disciplines, for example, political science, anthropology, psychology, economics and geography, and in the two decades after the Second World War such perspectives were increasingly applied to the Third World.

In many respects, the beginnings of modernization theory can be traced to antiquity, when the notion of evolution was first used with reference to human society. Certainly, the idea of progress is a continuing theme in Western intellectual thought. However, it was not until the eighteenth century that the evolution of societies was studied in a systematic way. As Bock remarks,

> a long, gradual process of social and cultural change considered as differentiation, a movement through defined stages from the simple to the complex, has marked Western social

1

thought throughout and dominated the great eighteenth-century program to establish a science of man and society (1979, p. 70).

Social evolutionism reached well into the nineteenth century, where it was reinforced by Darwin's work on biological evolution, and none of the early sociologists were free from this. In Western Europe, the nineteenth century was a time when people were aware that they were living through massive social changes which were radically altering the structures of society. As Bock has pointed out elsewhere (1964) nineteenth century theories of evolution were characterized by an emphasis on the naturalness and inevitability of such changes. It was the 'blockages' in evolution that required explanation, rather than the process itself. Change was seen to be continuous, slow, and manifest to all who possessed the necessary social scientific 'key' to understanding it. In so far as change occurred, it was deemed to follow the same pattern, and societies were distinguished from one another in that they occupied different positions on the evolutionary scale. The higher they moved up the scale the closer they became in type to Western industrial societies, and it should be noted that such societies were regarded by most writers (themselves of Western origin) as the highest known forms of civilization. Marx, for instance, spoke of 'laws', of 'tendencies working with iron necessity toward inevitable results', and suggested that 'the country that is more developed industrially only shows, to the less developed, the image of its own future' (Marx, 1954, p. 19).

Although there was considerable admiration for the achievements of Western industry and technology, the admiration was tinged with fear. The old order was being swept away and, with it, the security and predictability that seemed to characterize pre-industrial society. Indeed,

the fundamental ideas of European sociology are best understood as responses to the problem of order created at the beginning of the nineteenth century by the collapse of the old regime under the blows of industrialism and revolutionary democracy (Nisbet, 1966, p. 21).

2

Some of the main elements of nineteenth-century evolutionary theory can be seen in the work of Durkheim, especially in *The Division of Labour in Society* (1964, first published 1893). For him, pre-industrial societies, in particular, simple, unsegmented societies based on the horde or the clan, were typified by mechanical solidarity. In such societies, rules were based on an unstated but dominant consensus, the 'collective conscience', and individuals were similar to one another in crucial behavioural and moral respects. Social solidarity was borne out of likeness, resemblance and the unity of individual consciences, and it was mechanical because of the absolute domination of the collective conscience, which was based primarily on religious beliefs and sentiments. Durkheim viewed with considerable misgiving the rise of Western industrial society and the corresponding decline in the influence of the common conscience, and noted the increased heterogeneity, individualism and interdependence that arose from the division of labour. He considered that there were, in these developments, the seeds of a new moral order, and a social solidarity that was organic rather than mechanical. That said, he was also aware that evolution from one kind of social solidarity to another was not automatic; indeed, he felt that at the end of the nineteenth century, Western European societies evidenced an abnormal form of the division of labour. Lacking consensus, they were characterized by 'anomie', that is, rootlessness and a lack of regulation, and the moral order needed to be based on occupational associations which would provide individuals with moral discipline, with a sense of belonging, and which would encourage social solidarity and mutual assistance. In this way, the division of labour would be able to take over from the common conscience: 'It is the principal bond of social aggregates of higher types' (Durkheim, 1964, p. 173).

For Durkheim, then, societies evolve from lower to higher stages, and move from the simple and undifferentiated to the more complex. Western industrial society, with its highly developed division of labour, is ultimately superior to pre-industrial society, but only when it has dealt with the problems of social integration and value consensus. Taken together, these may be seen as the dominant themes of evolutionary theory which were to pass, through Durkheim and other nineteenth-century writers, into modernization theory. They were formulated at a time of rapid social and economic change, when traditional social orders were under attack and when the bases of new societies were yet to be established. They were revived after the Second World War, during a similar period of rapid socio-economic and political change. Then, however, it was the orderly evolution of the 'new nations' of the Third World which exercised the minds of the (predominantly Western) social scientists.

Evolutionism was but one of several influences on modernization theory. Indeed, even by the end of the nineteenth century, evolutionism was strongly challenged by the diffusionists, who sought to provide an alternative approach to social and cultural phenomena.

> Just as the idea of evolution referred to a genuine core phenomenon of progressive development, which occurred sometime in some places but not at all times in all places, so the idea of diffusion referred to the equally real transmission of cultural artefacts and other 'traits' from one region or community to another (Leaf, 1979, p. 164).

In North American anthropology, the notion of diffusion was associated with the rise of the Boas 'school' of ethnography. Generally, it came to be felt that evolutionist theories were inadequate in the explanation of social change. Their focus on one path of development was increasingly regarded as simplistic. In addition, the carnage of the First World War, in which millions were killed and wounded, dealt a severe blow to the smug assumption that Western culture and civilization were more advanced than elsewhere, and did little to confirm the view that technological supremacy was necessarily an advantage. The diffusionist perspective is based, in general, on the assumption that a common cultural pattern, or similar cultural artefacts, will have originated from a single source, and that innovation is likely to occur once only, rather than to be repeated by different groups at different times.

Whereas evolutionists focused on the transmission of culture over time, the diffusionists examined the way it was transferred in space via social interaction. Both perspectives encouraged a comparison of different cultures, but both also led to a great deal of unsupported speculation. It was hardly possible to subject the notion of stages of development to any empirical test, given the vast time spans involved, and a similar difficulty arose in discussions about the diffusion of cultural traits. To take a small, but later, example: when M and F Herskovits studied a Trinidadian village in the 1930s, they noted that eating habits were African, and that the men of the family ate meals before and apart from the women and children (1947, p. 289). In their view, this cultural trait clearly had been diffused from Africa. However, it had also been noted, at about that same time, by Arensberg and Kimball in rural Ireland, (1968, pp. 35-8; first published 1940) and thus the source of this particular cultural trait becomes less obvious. On a much larger scale, at the turn of the nineteenth century, it was actually suggested that all civilization had been diffused from ancient Egypt. Given this kind of generalization, it was not surprising that diffusionism became discredited. Isolated cultural traits, abstracted from their social context, were stripped of their significance in the continuing round of social life and forced to become components of highly fanciful explanations.

Despite the problems encountered in diffusionist explanations, diffusionism was to remain an important component in North American social science for some time. For a while, it seemed to have completely eclipsed evolutionism, and the two perspectives were often regarded as incompatible. For White, a committed evolutionist, the Boas school was wrong in contending that theories of cultural evolution had been disproved by the facts of diffusion. In his view, the early evolutionists were fully aware of diffusion, and it was the diffusionists who 'confused the evolution of culture with the culture history of peoples' (White, 1945, p. 343). Evolutionists did not insist that every social group had to go through every stage:

> The fact that a tribe gets a complex of traits from a foreign source of diffusion has nothing whatever to do with the series of stages in which this culture complex developed. Morgan and Tylor were well aware that tribes can and do take 'short cuts' via diffusion (White, 1945, p. 345).

As Evans-Pritchard noted (1962, pp. 17-18), diffusionism had less of an impact in Britain. In itself, this would be irrelevant, except for the fact that Parsons, one of the key figures in modernization theory, was strongly influenced by British social anthropology. Perhaps for this reason, the concept of diffusion did not figure to any large extent in his 'grand theory', but it was to become important in empirical studies of modernization, especially in attempts to understand how innovations were diffused.

For a time, evolutionism and diffusionism not only were regarded as mutually exclusive but also were considered to be alternatives to structural functionalism. The main tenets of modern structural functionalism are well known: societies are more or less self-sufficient, adaptive social systems, characterized by varying degrees of differentiation, and with roles and institutions, rather than concrete individuals, as their principal units. The balance, or equilibrium, of the various parts of the whole is maintained for as long as certain functional prerequisites are satisfied and, generally speaking, an institution is 'explained' once the functions it fulfils are satisfied. Finally, the entire system, or any part of it, is kept together through the operation of a central value system broadly embodying social consensus. That this kind of perspective need not be incompatible with evolutionism can be seen from Durkheim, who nevertheless was careful to distinguish between historical and functional elements in his explanations of social phenomena. As he puts it:

> To demonstrate the utility of a fact does not explain its origins, nor how it is what it is. The uses which it serves presume the specific properties characteristic of it, but do not create it (1982, p. 119-20).

In the opening decades of the twentieth century, evolutionism and diffusionism not only vied with each other for adherents, but also with structural functionalism, which was to become the dominant perspective in sociology and anthropology. Much of its increased influence was due to Malinowski, who was perhaps the first to develop structural functionalism as a specific approach to fieldwork. He insisted that to understand social life it is not enough to indulge in sociological abstraction. Instead, it is necessary to enter fully into the social situation we wish to understand, living with the indigenes, using their language, and not interpreters, joining in their happiness and sharing in their suffering. We had to become a part of their culture, and their culture had to become part of us. While Malinowski's fame now rests more on his empirical work, especially among the Trobriand islanders, among whom he was, in effect, interned during the First World War, he did try in his analysis to link individual needs to social and cultural needs. Initially, there are individual needs for food, drink, sleep and sex. These are reflected in the needs of all members of society for safety, bodily comfort, health and so on. At a cultural level, there are derived needs for reproduction through kinship and health through the practice of hygiene. This leads to yet another set of needs, in that societies, to survive, require economic systems to produce for and maintain their members, tools for production to occur, and goods for society's members to consume. In addition, social control is necessary, to regulate individual behaviour, along with education to socialize the young. Finally, political organization is also required to ensure that orders necessary for the continued existence of society are carried out. In this way, Malinowski moved, in fairly obvious stages, from the concept of basic needs of individuals to the derived needs that have to be met for the continued survival of entire societies and cultures.

This venture into Malinowski's structural functionalism is no mere historical digression, for his work was to have a profound influence on Talcott Parsons, one of the key figures in sociology and in post-1945 modernization theory. Indeed, it was with reference to Malinowski's four-fold classification of needs that Parsons was to remark that 'it can be treated as the master classification of functional imperatives of any social system or, indeed, of any system of action' (1957, p. 65). Many of the ingredients of this 'master classification' were embodied in Parsonian structural functionalism. As a result, an approach that arose from one of the earliest empirical studies of any Third World society entered into mainstream sociology of the 1950s and, in the process, contributed to one of the most abstract model of systems of action produced by any sociologist.

By the middle of the twentieth century, structural functionalists had come to dominate sociological theory and, among them, Talcott Parsons was pre-eminent. As Moore points out, a systems perspective has been evident not only in all explicitly functional analyses, but also in much analytical work that may leave theoretical assumptions mainly unstated, and in some scholarly work that explicitly adopts some form of conflict orientation (1979, p. 322).

In short, functionalism was the order of the day, and it was from the soil of Parsonian sociology that modernization theories sprouted. It is to this crop, in some of its major manifestations, that we now turn.

## Modernization Theory

In his inaugural address of 1949, President Truman announced the Point Four Programme of development aid, and subsequently it became

the policy of the United States to aid the efforts of the peoples of economically underdeveloped areas to develop their resources and improve their living conditions (Ohlin, 1970, p. 25).

As Ohlin and numerous others have pointed out this policy, which was hardly new, was not put forward out of altruism. Politically, the nations of the Third World were coming of age and, as far as the United States was concerned, they were flirting with undesirable elements, that is, the USSR. If modernization theory was planted in Parsonian soil, it was tended in a political climate dominated by the Cold War. And yet, at the time, many were optimistic that development aid was the answer to under-development. It is not surprising, then, that early treatments of development issues were somewhat ambivalent. The underlying fears, as well as much that made good sense, were expressed by several social scientists in *The Progress of Underdeveloped Areas*, edited by Bert F. Hoselitz in 1952. The book itself was a response to the Four Point programme and, although the authors came from a variety of disciplines and shared no specific theory, several themes emerged that were to be important for the following two decades. Their chief concern was the interrelationship of economic and cultural change and, more specifically, with the effects of Western technology on non-industrial societies. It was accepted that change in the economic sphere would lead to other, unanticipated, perhaps untoward, changes in the social, cultural and personality spheres. Innovation, diffusion, the introduction of technology from the outside and the role of traditional culture in 'blocking' development were continuing themes and so, too, was the 'threat' of Soviet influence if development – American style – were to fail. As social scientists, the general aim appeared to be (to quote a parallel source) 'to lessen the birth pangs' of that which had to be done. But it should not be supposed that such writers were blindly following an ideological line; contributors to the Hoselitz volume (1952) were well aware that the history of underdeveloped societies had often been one of colonialism and coercion, and it was commonly recognized that mono-causal theories of social change were inadequate. Nevertheless, the influence of colonialism did not figure as a major factor in this book; rather, it was implied that internal factors were the most crucial in determining whether or not development would take place. Indeed, the emphasis on internal factors, economic, social or cultural, was to characterize most modernization theory.

Like other contributors to the Hoselitz reader, Marion Levy (1952a) was primarily interested in what happened when Western technology was introduced into non-industrialized societies. However, unlike them he attempted to use a Parsonian perspective in his analysis, thus setting a precedent for many later studies. In particular, Levy focused on the pattern variables.

The pattern variables were first developed by Parsons because of his dissatisfaction with earlier studies of the ways in which social relationships had altered in the transition from non-industrial to industrial societies. In his view, such approaches had presented an over-simplified picture of social change, focusing as they did on two major variables. We have already seen, for example, that Durkheim emphasized the shift as one from mechanical to organic solidarity, and Parsons himself singled out the distinction made by Tonnies between relationships based on community (*Gemeinschaft*) and those based on association (*Gessellschaft*) (cf. Parsons and Shils, 1962, pp. 8-9). For Parsons and Shils, the pattern variables were basic dichotomies in role orientations. Every actor 'must make five specific dichotomous choices before any situation will have a determinate meaning' (1962, p. 76). These five choices, constituting a system, are the only ones possible. They are necessary, habitual, and internalized aspects of the wider value system. Actors have to decide whether to gratify an impulse or practise self-discipline (affect or affective neutrality); private or collective interests will be given priority (self-orientation or collective orientation); social objects, including other actors, will be treated in accord with general principles or according to their standing vis-à-vis the actor (universalism or particularism) and it has to be decided how far the actions of other individuals are to determine our sense of their worth (ascription or achievement). Finally, actors must decide which characteristics of other actors are deemed to be the most important when interacting with them (functional specificity or functional diffuseness).

At one stage, Parsons implied that, depending on how some of the pattern variables were grouped, it was possible to envisage four distinct kinds of social structure (Parsons, 1951, pp. 180-200). First, societies with open stratification systems, where status was closely correlated with occupational roles, where universalistic criteria predominated in a system of free exchange, and where individualism and high levels of consumer choice were found, were characterized as based on a universalistic-achievement pattern, considered to be favourable to Western industrialization. Secondly, and slightly less favourable (for example, pre-Nazi Germany and Soviet Russia), were those societies classified as universalistic-ascriptive. Here, status was based more on group membership and less on individual achievement, and there was a corresponding decline in social mobility. Thirdly, societies based on a particularist-achievement pattern placed little emphasis on generalized ideals. Instead, kinship dominated the occupational system and achievement was reduced to obtaining a position on a status hierarchy. As an example of this kind of society, Parsons cited Classical China. Finally, in a particularistic-ascriptive system there was no stress at all on achievement. All positions were ascribed and stability and tradition were highly valued. For Parsons, 'the Spanish-American seems to be a good example of this social type' (1951, p. 199).

A few years later, this classification was used, quite uncritically, by Spengler (1955, p. 379 ff.), who had somehow obtained the mistaken impression that Parson's scheme was 'based in part upon empirical findings' (1955, p. 380). However, the scheme played little part in Spengler's own analysis of the links between values and economic growth. In fact Levy, a former student of Parsons, was one of the first to take this framework for analysis, which for Parsons was primarily a series of ideal type constructs, and apply the pattern variables to the Third World:

When one looks at the social structure of relatively non-industrialized societies, with considerable uniformity one sees relationship patterns that emphasize traditional thinking, particularism, and functional diffuseness, and this would seem to be as marked with respect to the economic structure of those societies as with regard to others (Levy, 1952a, pp. 118-19).

More straightforwardly, Levy is suggesting that, in the Third World, social and economic interaction is generally underpinned by traditional values which emphasize the specific, known characteristics of interacting individuals, rather than the impersonal, formal, 'rational' criteria that allegedly operate in industrialized societies. Furthermore, he also implies that there is some kind of 'fit' between some role orientations and economic growth. Unlike non-industrial societies, developed societies evidence rationality, universalism and functional specificity, all of which are said to be necessary conditions for the efficient use of modern technology. In fact, it is a short step from this argument to suggest that, if only the basic role orientations of Third World actors were to become more like those that were prevalent in Western societies, economic growth would occur. 'They' would become more like 'us'.

A few years later, Hoselitz, an economist, also 'lifted' the pattern variables from Parsons and echoed Levy's conclusions. He, too, considered economic roles in underdeveloped countries to be particularistic, functionally diffuse, ascriptive and self-orientated (Hoselitz, 1960, pp. 29-42). However, it would be mistaken to attribute to him the belief that economic change was determined by social and cultural factors. Rather, he aimed to demonstrate that economic change cannot be explained by reference to economic factors alone. Referring to the pattern variables, he defends them against his fellow-economists:

This theoretical structure clearly omits, in the general form in which it is stated here, the purely economic variables significant for an explanation of the rise of average real output, such as capital formation and changes in the relative shares of primary and secondary industries associated with economic development. On the other hand it explicitly introduces a set of factors which economists almost always neglect or underestimate and which may be regarded as the primary social determinants of economic progress. Their neglect by economists was perhaps due to the fact that they are 'qualitative' and defy subjection to acknowledged standards of measurement. They can be stated therefore only as factors which are present to a greater or smaller degree and which have more or less significance for economic change (1960, p. 42).

The reference to 'social determinants of economic progress' makes it clear that, for Hoselitz, the economic, the social and the cultural are interrelated, and the inter-linkages and causal patterns vary across societies and according to the period in which development occurs. As far as the growth of Western capitalism is concerned, he takes a multi-causal approach, arguing that 'cultural and social-structural variables may be assumed to have created the conditions for economic change' (1960, p. 44). However, when it comes to recent Third World development, where economic change is more likely to be planned, the accumulation and mobilization of capital, new skills and modern technology are of primary importance. Here, social and cultural variables may be distinctly secondary: unable to cause economic growth, 'the social structure and culture imposes modifications of and, in some instances, barriers to the process of economic change' (1960, p. 44-5).

Hoselitz also attempted to deal with the transition from underdevelopment to development, and discussed at length the possibility that innovation in economic activity tends to be introduced by social deviants who, in some way or another, are marginal to the rest of society. The idea that entrepreneurs are often drawn from deviant minorities, from those who are denied 'normal' channels of making their way in society, was well established by the end of the 1950s (and has long been used to explain the role of Jews in commerce) and was to be taken up by several modernization theorists. For Hoselitz, the focus on deviants as innovators and entrepreneurs was interesting and relevant, 'a necessary but, in most cases, not a sufficient cause for social change' (1960, p. 68). He considered it was important, too, to examine other factors involved in development: the man/land ratio, for instance, which he felt helped determine the degree to which development would be expansionist or intrinsic. Where the former applied, economic frontiers might be extended by migrants, with or without coercion, whereas intrinsic development would be more likely to involve an intensification of economic activity within a given geographical area. A similar distinction between internal and external factors had been made by Levy (1952a, p. 114), who, like Hoselitz, concentrated primarily on internal causes of development. However, Hoselitz went on to relate the process of development to political structures, suggesting that expansionism was more likely to occur in, and reinforce, a relatively open stratification system, whereas intrinsic change tended to reinforce rigid class structures and centralized decision making.

It has been argued that Hoselitz ignored the overriding economic and political structures within which underdevelopment is situated (Frank, 1969, p. 37) and undoubtedly the influence of colonialism was underplayed. However, he does not ignore it entirely, as at least one reference to Latin America makes clear (1960, p. 246). Then follows a passage that, with minor modifications, could have been written by a neo-Marxist critic of modernization theory, anxious to demonstrate the barriers erected by international capitalism to independent capitalist development in the Third World:

> It is undeniable that the dominant status group will attempt to prevent the development of a middle sector and will try to draw individuals in the emerging middle class under its influence. For an independent middle class, especially one with *independent, self-determined economic sources of social strength*, forms a danger to the leading political and status group which has every interest to prevent or counteract this development (1960, p. 246; my emphasis).

It is easy to criticize Hoselitz for the naivety with which he applied the pattern variables, for the minor role he gave to colonialism and military power and, indeed, for his stress on elites

(1960, p. 75 ff). However, he was not without merit: he warned against the view that underdeveloped societies would follow European paths of development, emphasized the importance of research into development in specific societies, and attempted to relate economic change to social, cultural and political variables. His interest in non-economic factors associated with development was reflected in the establishment, in the early 1950s, of the journal *Economic Development and Cultural Change*. All of this was no mean achievement for an economist writing at a time when 'new states' were still being formed, and who was using sociological concepts when sociologists themselves had paid so little attention to the Third World.

Much the same might be said of the contribution of Riggs, a political scientist writing at the same time as Hoselitz. In Riggs (1964) the influence of Parsons and Levy was again evident. Focusing especially on functional specificity, one of the pattern variables, Riggs pointed out that the economic and social structures of transitional societies were such that it was normally impossible to genuinely reproduce Western institutions. Using terms borrowed from optical science, he suggests that whereas traditional, or 'fused' societies are homogeneous, and modern, or 'diffracted' societies are highly differentiated, transitional societies are neither one nor the other. Like a prism, receiving white light from one source and diffracting it in numerous directions and colours, they contain elements, in widely differing combinations, of both the received and the diffracted light. It is in this sense that they are prismatic. Put more simply, transitional societies are not what they seem. Their formal political structures, superimposed on them by the West, only appear modern. In fact, political elites exercise power unrestricted by those counteracting institutions operating in the West, and there is a lack of normative consensus. Widely differing and hostile communities and cultural groups compete for power and influence and the bureaucracy, in these circumstances, and despite its formal rational-legal veneer, serves as a vehicle for self-interest and corruption, with the bureaucrats themselves actively manipulating the system for their own ends.

Whilst Riggs was primarily interested in administration in the Third World, there is in his work a more general recognition that what he has to say about political and administrative structures may also apply to other spheres of social life. He was undoubtedly influenced by Parsons and the pattern variables, but this did not prevent him from going further than Parsons or Levy in examining the pent-up conflict and contradictions that may arise when Western patterns of public administration and government are superimposed on traditional societies. As a consequence, although he is often regarded as a modernization theorist, his work has also been considered relevant by critics of modernization theory (cf. Cruise O'Brien, 1979, p. 57 ff.). It is perhaps because he did not espouse any general theoretical approach to development and underdevelopment that he can be claimed by both camps. That said, his concerns have not been taken up by either and, indeed, at the time Riggs was writing there was no such general perspective. In so far as he was influenced by Parsons and Levy, his insights were obtained from texts that applied structural functionalist models to all societies. At that time, there was no specific sociological approach to the Third World.

## Early Empirical Studies

So far, I have referred to the first, faltering steps in the development of modernization theory. Later, in the 1960s, evolutionism was to make something of a come-back, and there were also significant contributions from other sociological perspectives. At this point, however, it would perhaps be relevant to indicate how these early theoretical concerns were reflected in empirical studies of the Third World, because in the late 1950s and early 1960s there was no shortage of political will to fund such studies. In the wider context, they were prompted by the independence of India and Pakistan and, later, of other 'new states', and the foreign aid programme of the United States ensured that considerable research funds were available. Attention was often directed to the numerous barriers tradition allegedly presented to those who wished to introduce technological change (Foster, 1962). Others examined the degree to which tradition and modernity, seen usually as ideal types, were compatible (Randolph and Randolph, 1967), and yet others, following established economic theory, studied the nature and social origins of innovators and entrepreneurs. It would be mistaken to assume that all of this

15

was unique to the Third World; indeed, much of it originated in work carried out in the West. When Rogers (1962), in a particularly influential book, summarized more than 500 accounts of the diffusion of innovation, the vast majority of his examples were taken from the USA. And yet it seemed that if the causes of innovation and diffusion were relevant to the United States, a 'developed country', they were even more relevant to the Third World, and later Rogers extended his interest further afield (Solo and Rogers, eds, 1972).

One of the most famous of early modernization studies was carried out by Daniel Lerner. In *The Passing of Traditional Society* (1958) he examined the process of modernization in several Middle East countries, carried out a sample survey in other underdeveloped societies, and supplemented all this with observations of village society. The picture painted by Lerner is of a world in which modernization is a global process, the same the world over. Traditional society is on the wane, and Islam is 'defenceless' against the 'rationalist and positivist spirit' (p. 45). In particular, the role of the mass media is crucial, and is associated with a cluster of other indices of development: urbanization, accompanied by an increase in literacy, leads to an increase in exposure to the mass media. At the same time, the increasingly literate and urbanized population participates in a wider economic system. For Lerner, modernity comes about through changes not only in institutions but also in persons, and he vividly illustrates this in his account of the grocer and the chief in the village of Balgat.

In 1950, when it was first visited by one of Lerner's interviewers, the village of Balgat, in Turkey, appeared to have no future. Lacking a decent road, isolated from the outside world, with only one radio, it was dominated by its chief. He owned the radio (to which he gave selected villagers a carefully rationed access) and he was clearly the guardian of traditional virtues of bravery, loyalty and obedience. At the other end of the social scale was the grocer, the village's only merchant and non-farmer. Although he had been to Ankara, and occasionally advised villagers planning a visit on the best coffee houses to frequent and the most exciting films to see, the grocer was considered a disreputable character. He openly admitted he wanted a better life than the village could offer, stated his individuality by wearing a necktie, and dreamed of owning an American-style shop in Ankara. Clearly he was a fool and a heretic.

Four years later, when Lerner visited Balgat, it had a new road and a regular bus service. Indeed, it was now a sub-district of Ankara. The men of the village were no longer farmers; instead, most worked for wages in Ankara's factories, earning far more than they could have earned in agricultural labour, and as a consequence food had to be imported into Balgat. Money was also spent on radios, of which there were now about a hundred, and (the chief and his womenfolk complained) the young men of the village were becoming disrespectful and forward towards the young village women. However, the chief's sons were neither soldiers nor farmers (which he would have preferred) but shopkeepers, thus realizing, in part, the dream of the grocer who, regrettably, had died in the period between 1950 and 1954.

For Lerner, the story of the grocer and the chief is a modern parable, and one which encapsulates the world-wide process of modernization. We might wish to be less enthusiastic than Lerner in our assessment of the changes which occurred in Balgat between 1950 and 1954 and, with the benefit of hindsight, we might be less inclined to dismiss Islam as 'defenceless'. Certainly, the decline in local food production is difficult to justify, and the new-found confidence of young Balgati males was, at best, a mixed blessing. However, the parable is really a prelude to the more general issues raised in Lerner's study. For him, one of the crucial aspects of modernization is the development of a 'mobile personality', characterized by rationality and empathy, which 'enables newly mobile persons to *operate efficiently* in a changing world. Empathy, to simplify the matter, is the capacity to see oneself in the other fellow's situation' (Lerner, 1958, p. 49-50 ; author's emphasis).

According to Lerner, the capacity to empathize predominates in modern society, where it is encouraged and, to a considerable degree taught, by the mass media – a 'mobility multiplier'. Modernization, then, is characterized by a high degree of literacy, urbanism, media participation and empathy. Learner classified individual respondents to his questionnaires as traditional, transitional or modern. From the responses, he found that, compared with 'traditional' individuals, the 'moderns' were happier, better informed, and relatively young. People placed in the intermediate category of 'transitional' were inclined to be discontented and liable to extremism, especially if their progress was blocked by a lack of suitable political institutions.

Although Lerner assumes that the process of development is both good and inevitable, and sometimes implies that his 'moderns' are actually more virtuous than their traditional counterparts, he was aware that development did not occur without difficulties. Strains are placed on governmental institutions, and there may be problems of social control.

In addition, he recognizes that at an individual level there will be crises of identity, especially at the 'transitional' phase, where people somehow have to adjust traditional Arab and Moslem beliefs to a 'modern' setting.

Several themes common to early modernization theory are found in Lerner's study: the classification of societies as traditional or modern, albeit with an intermediate category; a focus on such indices of modernity as urbanization and literacy; exposure to the diffusing influence of the mass media; the importance given to specific personality types in the process of modernization. In addition, the implicitly evolutionist perspective, and the view of modernization as the infusion of a 'rationalist or positivist spirit' owe much to an understanding, or misunderstanding, of Weber's work on the Protestant ethic.

As with many questionnaires used in sample surveys, it is debatable how far stated opinion is actually reflected in social action, and it is also questionable whether or not modernization, which is equated with Westernization, should be presumed at the outset to be beneficial. Certainly, to suggest that tradition is unable to withstand modernity is sweeping enough, even without the evaluation contained within the evolutionist perspective. It might also be argued that Lerner ignored economic structures and the international context in which modernization was occurring, and there is no doubt that neo-Marxist critics would be less favourably inclined than Lerner towards the mass media. However, this does not make the focus on individual agents of change invalid. The grocer of Balgat with his 'modern', if somewhat outlandish, ideas is a very real figure, whose counterparts can be found all over the Third World. Undoubtedly, conclusions are begged about the ways in which people become modern (and what the term really means) but the point is that values, and their relationship to the wider community, are significant factors in discussions of development.

The question of values was also taken up by McClelland, a psychologist who for many years studied how people came to evince a 'need for achievement', otherwise known as n.ach. By this, McClelland means 'the desire to do something better, faster, more efficiently, with less effort'. (1976, p.A) Those who evidence this trait are similar in some respects to Lerner's mobile personalities. In brief, McClelland asserts that the need for achievement can be found in individuals from different cultures, and that this need is associated with other indices of development, including economic growth. As a personality attribute, or 'mental virus', n.ach. is developed in children through literature that emphasizes the value of self-help, competition, and generally outgoing behaviour. Clearly, a country that wishes to encourage an entrepreneurial spirit could inculcate its young, at the correct age, of course, with those values associated with the need for achievement. However, adults, too, are able to develop this personality trait, and McClelland claimed that short training courses for Indian businessmen had demonstrated that within a few days they became more adventurous, innovative, enterprising and generally more efficient. He does not entirely ignore social factors, and accepts that the need for achievement is not the only ingredient in modernization. Historical factors are also important in determining whether or not specific groups evidence the trait. In addition, he claims that people who are especially zealous in reformist religions are also more likely to possess n.ach., a suggestion which, like other elements in his approach, is strongly reminiscent of the notion of a culture of poverty, as put forward by Oscar Lewis (1966) which also could be overcome by religious or political conversion.

Finally, at a psychological level, economic success is seen, by McClelland, as constructed on a desire to prove superiority and to promote the common good. Nevertheless, such a desire can be produced in a variety of ways, including specific training programmes introduced primarily to promote the growth of the need for achievement.

As Goldthorpe remarks (1975, p. 227), 'it is difficult to escape the impression that the ideas of McClelland and his colleagues are not entirely free from ethnocentricism'. Indeed, this may be something of an understatement, and Frank is typically more forthright in suggesting that one conclusion that seems to follow from McClelland's work, and from that of others like him, is that 'the present economic, social and political structure does not matter at all: there is no need to change the status quo' (Frank, 1969, p. 74). A society that encourages competitiveness and self-help among the very young, that pushes the achievement mystique at every available opportunity, that trains businessmen to develop their need for achievement and their interest in the common good (measured, perhaps, in profits?) and, in addition, is prepared to grant credit and other assistance to such businessmen, surely bears more than a passing resemblance to the United States, or to a United States that many people fondly imagine to exist. It is one thing to isolate selected personality characteristics, but quite another to credit them with such importance.

Whereas the influence of Weber in the work of Lerner was implicit, McClelland linked his own focus on the need for achievement quite explicitly with Weber's famous study of the role of Protestantism, especially the Puritan sects, in the development of capitalism (McClelland, 1976, pp. 47-53). Weberian influence may also be detected in the study of attitudes to modernity carried out by Inkeles and Smith over several years and finally published in book form in 1974. On the basis of some 6,000 interviews, that took place in six underdeveloped countries over a ten-year period, they find evidence of an 'Overall Modernity' syndrome. 'Modern Man' (who appears to be without modern woman) is truly modern when he has changed as an individual, and modernity is indicated by the presence of a distinct set of attitudes, which may be summarized as follows:

(1) A readiness for new experience and an openness to innovation;
(2) An interest in things other than those of immediate relevance;
(3) A more 'democratic' attitude towards the opinions of others;
(4) An orientation to the future rather than the past;
(5) A readiness to plan one's own life;
(6) A belief that we can dominate our environment and achieve our goals;

(7)   An acceptance that the world is 'calculable' and therefore controllable;

(8)   An awareness of the dignity of others, for example, women and children;

(9)   A faith in the achievement of science and technology, albeit a somewhat simple faith; finally

(10)  A belief in 'distributive' justice.

It may be that such a list could only have been produced in the 1960s, for it is certainly ill-at-ease in the 1980s, when 'democracy' is often what is practised by 'our' side, when control and dignity are denied to millions, and when faith in the achievements of science and technology is, to say the least, somewhat tarnished. Nevertheless, from even a cursory examination of the alleged characteristics of 'modern man', it should be evident that many of them have been associated with the development of Western rationality, as seen in the writing of Max Weber. Indeed, it is questionable, according to these criteria, how 'modern' many who live in the West really are. However, Inkeles and Smith found several factors to be important in the development of modernity, including (again) education and exposure to the mass media and, in particular, experience of work in the modern factory which, they maintain, *exemplifies* efficiency' (1974, p. 158; authors' emphasis).

Psychological studies of modernization do not necessarily rely on insights derived from Weber. When Hagen, for instance, attempted to explain the reasons for economic growth (1962), he based his approach on Erikson's personality theory (Erikson, 1950). Nevertheless, Weber's famous thesis on the influence of the puritan sects on the development of capitalism (Weber, 1930) has clearly been influential in many explanations of social and economic change. He attempted to explain why capitalism arose, at the time it did, in Western Europe, especially England. Although Weber is aware that the spirit of capitalism existed before this period, he asserts that the rationalization of economic attitudes, along with the idea that individuals were duty bound to be diligent in their work, was given a major impetus by Puritanism, especially Calvinism. Work became a vocation, a 'calling', and success in business came to be seen as evidence of spiritual salvation. The religious prohibition of earthly pleasures seemed to reinforce this tendency. Put rather simply, if profit could not be spent on wine, women and song, it could be ploughed back into the business. Compared with this rigorous approach to work and religion, traditional Christianity, with its array of mediators between humanity and God, was more comfortable, less inclined to cast doubt on an individual's salvation, and certainly did not regard business or industry as particularly worthy spheres of service to the Almighty. And Weber also attempted to demonstrate that traditional, non-Christian religions were not conducive to the growth of the spirit of capitalism. For him, what was of crucial importance, but not the sole explanation for capitalism, was the difference in attitude between traditionalists and the new capitalists. Undoubtedly, economic changes were important. Capitalism required rational calculation in money terms, a free labour force and a universalistic legal system with formal rules (all of which are also emphasized by Parsons), but most of all it required a change in attitude, a new spirit and innovators who were calculating, daring and 'above all temperate and reliable, shrewd and completely devoted to their business, with strictly bourgeois opinions and principles' (Weber, 1930, p. 69). Once this new spirit was accepted, legitimated by, and an unintended consequence of, Puritanism, capitalism was able to cast aside the obstacles of tradition. In short, it 'took off', albeit from an economic launching pad.

Although the Weber thesis has had its critics (cf. Green, 1973; Marshall, 1982), it exerted a powerful influence on modernization theory. Often it was applied quite uncritically to the Third World, even though, as I shall demonstrate later, there were social scientists who took a less simplistic approach to the relationship between tradition and modernity. However, many early modernization studies focused on one or two key factors in the process of modernization, and few attempted to provide a more general framework for analysing social change in the Third World.

## Smelser and Rostow

Both Smelser and Rostow attempted to provide more general perspectives in the analysis of development. Smelser, a sociologist, was particularly concerned with the effects of economic development (by which he seems to have meant economic growth) on social structures. He detailed four major processes that were especially important. First, there was a move from simple to complex technology, secondly, a change from subsistence farming to cash crops, thirdly, a move from animal and human power to industrialization and, finally, an increasingly urban-based population. Smelser stressed that such processes would not occur simultaneously, and that changes would differ from one society to another. There was a variety of 'pre-modern' starting points and the impetus to change would also vary, being crucially affected by tradition, thus leading to different paths towards modernization. He went on to suggest that national differences are always important, even in the most advanced stages of modernization, and also noted that 'dramatic events', for example, wars and natural disasters, can crucially affect the pattern of development.

At first sight it would appear that Smelser is moving cautiously. However, he goes on to suggest that, local conditions notwithstanding, these four processes of change have a similar effect on modernizing societies. First, structural differentiation occurs, a process whereby

> *One* social role or organization ... differentiates into *two or more* roles or organizations which function more effectively in the new historical circumstances. The new social units are structurally distinct from each other, but taken together are functionally equivalent to the original unit (Smelser, 1969; author's emphasis).

In other words, the family 'loses' functions, economic activities become distinct from domestic and religious spheres and social stratification becomes more complex, with greater emphasis on achievement and social mobility.

Secondly, to maintain social cohesiveness, new integrative mechanisms arise. Welfare agencies link the family to the economy, voluntary associations emerge, including trades unions, to counter feelings of anonymity brought about by urbanization, and new political institutions cater for an increasing number of interest groups. All of this is quite in line with a structural functionalist perspective that emphasizes the 'adaptive' capacity of societies and the corresponding need for social equilibrium.

Despite the formation of new integrative mechanisms, Smelser regards 'social disturbances' as inevitable. They come about for several reasons, the most important of which are the clash of tradition and modernization, unevenness of structural change and the rapidity of industrialization. In effect, modernizing societies are portrayed as battlegrounds, where tradition is pitted against the forces of structural differentiation and where integrative mechanisms strive to hold the balance. The success of these mechanisms depends, amongst other things, on the intensity of structural change, the nature of pre-modern society, the degree to which the rebels have access to political power, the extent to which rival social groups overlap and, finally, the amount of foreign intervention.

Overall, it is difficult to escape the conclusion that Smelser is dealing with a more or less uniform pattern of social change, in which modernizing societies are following the example set by their more advanced counterparts. And social adaptation seems to occur without a great deal of assistance from human agents. Instead, societies are like gigantic self-correcting machines, with defence mechanisms being brought into play as soon as social equilibrium is threatened. That said, he does not pretend that modernization is easy, or that industrialization, the springboard of economic growth, will occur immediately.

Some of the most far-reaching structural changes have occurred in countries where industrialization has hardly begun. For instance, colonialism or related forms of economic dominance create not only an extensive differentiation of cash products and wage-labor, but also a vulnerability to world price fluctuations in commodities. Hence many of the structural changes already described, and the consequent social disturbances to be described presently, are characteristics of societies which are still technically pre-industrial (Smelser, 1969, p. 56).

Industrialization may have 'hardly begun', but the implication is that, in the end, it will come, provided that social disturbances can be dealt with. Social and political instability will perhaps be inevitable, either because of rapid economic growth or, alternatively, because industrialization is not proceeding fast enough. In these circumstances, it may be necessary for 'strong, centralized government' (1969, p. 60) to emerge, perhaps using nationalism as a rallying point, thus enhancing its own legitimacy, obtaining sacrifices from the populace and increasing its ability to repress protests 'and prevent generalized symbols, such as communism, from spreading to all sorts of particular grievances' (1969, p. 61).

Many people in underdeveloped societies, with ideologies of the 'Left' as well as the 'Right', have made similar calls for firm leadership, always provided, of course, that such leadership espouses their own particular cause. Clearly, 'strong, centralized government' is a term that can cover a multitude of sins, and there can be little doubt of Smelser's own ideological orientation. However, his work is also open to criticism on other grounds, not least because of its somewhat mechanistic depiction of social change. Nevertheless, he makes it clear that he is referring to social change in ideal-typical terms (1969, p. 43), and it is equally clear, although implied, that the change is from 'traditional' to 'modern'. It is more relevant, perhaps, to suggest that his four major processes of economic and technological change, and their social effects, are virtually identical to those deemed to have occurred in the industrialized West. One need go no further than Durkheim to discover many of them. Once again, conclusions derived from the study of development in the West have been applied to the Third World.

In Smelser, we have a kind of neo-Durkheimian, structural functionalist perspective, which sees social change in the Third World as a necessary factor in economic growth. If only social disturbances can be contained, perhaps through new, stronger political institutions and leadership, the Third World will be able to emulate the Western path, albeit with some local variations. The alleged 'fit' between economic and social development is even more evident in the work of Rostow, an economic historian also interested in social change. His importance to the sociology of development lies, first, in the promise he holds out of rapid economic development for the Third World, if only the barriers of tradition can be overcome and, secondly, and perhaps more importantly, in the weight that his views came to have, for a time, in the political arena in the United States. His economics and his political opinions, especially during the Vietnam War, have attracted the opprobrium of the Left, and it is not difficult to see why. Indeed, there have been times when an attack on

Rostow's politics has been a necessary and sufficient condition for the discrediting of his more academic theories.

In his best known publication (1960), Rostow suggests that all societies can be placed in one of five categories, or stages of economic growth. These he derives from his study of Western economic development. In traditional society, the first stage, output is limited because of the inaccessibility of science and technology. Values are generally fatalistic and political power is non-centralized. At the second stage, 'the preconditions for take-off', new ideas favouring economic progress arise and, with them, education, entrepreneurship, and institutions capable of mobilizing capital. Investments increase, especially in transport, communication and raw materials, and the result is a general commercial expansion. Nevertheless, despite the development of some modern manufacturing, traditional social structures and production techniques remain. In effect, we have a dual society:

> In many cases, for example, the traditional society persisted side by side with modern economic activities, conducted for limited economic purposes by a colonial or quasi-colonial power (Rostow, 1960, p. 7).

For Rostow, the pre-conditions for take-off were endogenous in Britain, whereas elsewhere they were more likely to have been the result of 'external intrusion by more advanced societies' (1960, p. 6).

Rostow's third stage is 'the Take-Off', where traditional barriers to economic growth are overcome, perhaps through the absorption of new technology alone (as in Britain and its Dominions) or with the additional emergence of new political groups, prepared to accord a high priority to the modernization of the economy. Investment increases rapidly and new industries expand, as does the entrepreneurial class. Agriculture, too, is commercialized, with a corresponding growth in productivity, a necessary development if the demand emanating from expanding urban centres is to be met.

At the fourth stage, 'the Drive to Maturity', between 10 and 20 per cent of national income is invested and the economy takes its place in the international order. Technology becomes more complex and there is a move away from heavy industry.

What is produced is now less a matter of economic necessity, more a question of choice. This leads to the final stage, of high consumption, where the leading economic sectors specialize in manufacturing durable consumer goods and services. Basic needs are satisfied and there is a focus on social welfare and security. According to Rostow, in the United States this stage was heralded by the mass production of the motor car.

Rostow presents us with a theory, which he claims to be dynamic, dealing not only with economic factors but also with 'social decisions and policies of governments' (1960, p. 15). Like other modernization theorists, he incorporates the notion of diffusion in his account of development: although the European powers did not 'maximise the creation of the pre-conditions for take-off', they did move societies along the appropriate path and 'often included modernization of a sort as one object of colonial policy' (1960, p. 112). a statement which appears to justify colonialism. Like Marion Levy, he regarded the process of modernization as more or less inevitable: in theory, societies could opt to halt development but in practice the momentum would be maintained by population increase and the ever-increasing attractions of modern living standards. Finally, like some more recent modernization theorists, he suggested that, at any given time, the available technology inevitably set constraints upon social, economic and political action but that, within these constraints, individuals were free to make significant choices. Later, in response to his critics, Rostow made it clear he did not rule out political and social intervention; however, 'the range of choices at any particular time is, as always, framed and limited by the resources a society can mobilize and the imperatives of the technologies it desires to absorb' (Rostow, 1971, p. 177).

Since it was first put forward, Rostow's theory of the stages of growth has been much criticized, sometimes gently (Rostow, 1963 and 1971) and sometimes vehemently. (Frank, 1969, p. 39 ff.) Leaving aside purely economic arguments, it is doubtful if Western development really occurred along the lines he suggests, and even more unlikely that it could occur on such lines in the Third World. As Gunder Frank remarks, such an ideal-typical approach, 'in all its variations, ignores the historical and structural reality of the under-developed countries' (1969, p. 47). In short, far from colonialism helping to modernize the Third World, it served to hinder its development. If this is indeed the case (and it is the nub of underdevelopment theory), the political message emanating from Rostow's work is even more inappropriate: if colonialism and neo-colonialism have actively under-developed the Third World, it is unlikely that closer association with, and emulation of, the United States, will enable Third World countries to make up the ground they have lost in the race towards the age of high consumption.

It may be that, stripped of its political appeal, Rostow's importance has been exaggerated. Indeed, in discussing a more recent work (Rostow, 1978), a distinguished critic claims that even among economists Rostow's influence has been overestimated:

> What remains is a dream world in which economic growth proceeds in all units in the same linear manner, though with an earlier or later start and at different speeds, each economy's position on the Rostovian cross-country track through the prescribed (and largely tautologous) 'stages of growth' being clearly marked and graded (Hobsbawm, 1979, p. 307).

Rostow's theory undoubtedly shares some of the characteristics of other modernization theorists. His unilinear approach to development, and the idea that traditional societies not only had to change their economies but also their values and social structures, can be found elsewhere. Indeed, it was but a short step from here to suggest, or to imply, that alterations in values could automatically lead to changes in economic structures. In other words: remove cultural blockages and somehow economic development would take care of itself, perhaps with the help of a modernizing elite and a little diffusion from outside.

Whereas Smelser considered 'strong, centralized government' a necessity, and Rostow emphasized entrepreneurial elites in the period of economic 'take-off', such themes were general among early modernization theorists. Indeed, Lipset's discussion of elites in Latin America encapsulates some of the key concepts of modernization theory, including yet another reference to the pattern variables. He notes that

> the available materials from many Latin American countries seem to agree that the predominant values which continue to

inform the behaviour of the elite stem from the continued and combined strength of ascription, particularism and diffuseness (Lipset, 1967, p. 12).

Summarizing the available empirical studies of Latin America, Lipset finds that a non-entrepreneurial spirit pervades 'aristocratic' values, and that compared with the USA at it. own 'take-off', immigrants were heavily and disproportionately represented among Latin American entrepreneurs. Indeed, '...regardless of the causal pattern one prefers to credit for Latin American values, they are, as described, antithetic to the basic logic of a large-scale industrial system' (Lipset, 1967, p. 32).

His solutions for this sad state of affairs may be described as revolutionary and reformist. The revolutionary solution was the overthrow of those in power who continued to insist on the primacy of traditional values and their replacement by modern, more entrepreneurial elites. However, there was also a reformist solution, perhaps seen as an alternative to this drastic measure, in which formal educational curricula were changed to emphasize vocational criteria, problem-solving and achievement in all disciplines, especially in science and technology. In this way, traditional value systems need not be rejected, provided methods can be found to ensure that members of the elite and recruits from outside this stratum are motivated to study subjects which will allow them to develop their entrepreneurial and innovative skills. As Lipset notes, such proposals may run contrary to many entrenched interests and 'considerable innovative skills may have to be applied to overcome such opposition' (Lipset, 1967, p. 49).

*Summary*

By this stage, the main tenets of modernization theory up to the mid 1960s should be evident. They can be summarized quite briefly:

(1) In many respects, modernity and tradition were regarded as antithetical. People, values, institutions and societies were either traditional or modern. They could not be both,

and when the two came together there would inevitably be some kind of 'social disturbance'. At best, there was an uneasy symbiosis, probably of a temporary nature, in which modern and traditional institutions might co-exist in a 'dual society'. In more human terms, the grocer could live alongside the chief – but not for long.

(2)  Early modernization theory placed special stress on factors internal to specific societies. Generally, these were the 'wholes' which were the subject of structural functionalist analysis, and it was the role of values, of culture, especially religion, which was of most interest to modernization theory. Among the values alleged to predominate in Third World societies were those associated with the traditional, pre-industrial pattern variables developed by Parsons, that is, ascription, functional diffuseness and particularism. It was not normally felt that economic growth sprang directly from 'modern' values, but more often than not tradition was seen as a barrier to growth. Put rather simply, values were embodied in culture, and culture frequently blocked development (that is, economic growth); it then followed that if the barriers to development could be removed, or minimized, growth would occur, both through the unleashing of an entrepreneurial spirit within the society and through the diffusion of modernity from outside. It must be said that the world outside was largely unspecified. By implication, it was divided into two camps, that which was friendly (the USA and its allies) and that which, however benign it appeared, wanted to involve itself in the Third World for its own nefarious purposes, that is, the USSR.

(3)  Interest in specific groups or classes in the Third World was concentrated on those considered to be 'change agents'. At an individual level, they were 'mobile personalities', in possession of a 'need to achieve'; they were the 'moderns'. Structurally, they were relatively well educated, more responsive to the mass media, and probably urban-based or 'cosmopolitan' in their orientation. In some societies they were drawn disproportionately from minorities, from groups less bound by tradition, but everywhere there was a need for a 'modernizing elite', willing and institutionally able, albeit through 'strong government', to shake sleepy,

ascriptive, non-rational Third World societies into the period of economic 'take-off' and beyond. According to this perspective, development was undoubtedly from above.

(4)   It was the 'change agents' who were likely to be innovators or (more probably) to diffuse new ideas obtained from elsewhere. Innovation and diffusion are clearly linked, logically and in practice, and in one sense it matters little whether a new culture trait originates within or from outside a society. Those who take the lead in putting this trait into practice may be regarded as innovators, and in the process they will (it is hoped) also act as diffusers. However, in early modernization theory it was invariably implied that the ideas, practices, technology or capital that were to be diffused in any Third World society originated outside the Third World. The trait, institution, or capital would be adopted by a change agent, adapted to suit the new cultural environment and actively diffused throughout the society, not without benefits to change agents themselves. Indeed, in the 1950s and 1960s, numerous manuals were issued by United Nations agencies, instructing fieldworkers on how to identify innovators and increase their importance and influence.

(5)   Innovators, diffusers, or change agents, were, in effect, the human mechanisms through which societies 'adapted' to meet the challenge of modernity. It was taken for granted that change was both inevitable and worthwhile and that, once commenced, it would continue under its own momentum. It was also assumed that, by and large, and allowing for differences in 'pre-modern' societies, the direction of change would tend to be the same for all Third World societies, much along the lines of that which had already occurred in the West.

(6)   It should be evident that evolutionism, diffusionism and structural functionalism all contributed to the theoretical 'mix' that constituted early modernization theory, and that this was based especially on the structural functionalism of Talcott Parsons and his related concepts of the pattern variables, both of which had been developed in general sociological analysis and neither of which were designed for particular application to the Third World. Because of

this theoretical orientation, and the fact that the 'wholes' of the analysis tended to be actual societies, it is clear that the influence of factors outside these societies was given little prominence. Colonialism, and all this implies, may not have been totally ignored, but it is hardly the case that the relationships of the Third World with the West or with the Eastern bloc loomed large in the analysis. By the same token, the view of Third World societies as relatively self-contained systems meant that the causes of under-development were seen, in general, to rest within their own structures, and were attributed to their own deficiencies. It then followed that, if they were to develop, the main focus of remedial attention would have to be those internal characteristics; somehow they would have to be adjusted to bring about a greater 'fit' with industrialization and modernity.

The above tenets are open to severe criticism, and even in the mid-1960s there were sociologists, for example, Bendix, who cast doubt on their major assumptions. Such objections will be considered in more detail in the following chapters. However, before this it is necessary to understand how modernization theory was reinforced in the 1960s by a revival in evolutionary perspectives led, as we might expect, by Talcott Parsons.

# 2

# Neo-Evolutionism and Modernization Theory

## *Parsons and Neo-Evolutionism*

In the work of such modernization theorists as Lerner, Inkeles and Smith, and Smelser, along with Hoselitz, Rostow and McClelland, there was frequently an appeal to a type of evolutionism that was more implicit than explicit. This was to change, in 1964, with the publication of an issue of the *American Sociological Review*, which was devoted to a re-appraisal of evolutionary theory. In general, the contributors to this volume agreed in several basic respects:

(1) Societies are adaptive systems that are geared to survival;
(2) They are primarily normative systems;
(3) Innovation and diffusion are crucial in modernization, and
(4) Modern societies are unique, especially in the extent of their internal differentiation.

Given this consensus, however, the articles vary considerably in scope and the level of abstraction. Although Moore purports to discuss the possibilities for prediction in sociology, his main concern appears to be to modify any tendency among neo-evolutionists to assume uni-directionality and consistency in evolution. Social change is thus characterized by 'reversals', 'cycles and swings', the 'completion of processes', the 'partial restoration' of earlier structural features, 'fluctuations' and 'structural substitution' (Moore, 1964, pp. 334-6). Nevertheless, Moore remained a cautious evolutionist. This cannot be said of Parsons, whose theorizing on the subject was more comprehensive and who can be taken, at least for present purposes, as the representative, or 'exemplar', of neo-evolutionary theory.

Drawing parallels from organic evolution, Parsons suggested that for societies to move from the primitive to the modern, several 'evolutionary universals' have to be present. By this, he means

> any organizational development sufficiently important to further evolution that, rather than emerging only once, it is likely to be 'hit upon' by various systems operating under different conditions (1964, p. 339).

Elsewhere, he defines an evolutionary universal as 'any complex of structures and processes which so increases the long-run adaptive capacity of living systems' (1964, p. 340-1).

According to Parsons, for a human society to exist at all, certain 'prerequisites' must be met, that is, religion, communication with language, social organization through kinship and technology. These are the basic, and universal, requirements of any human society. It should be noted that, for Parsons, 'culture implies the existence of technology, which is, in its most undifferentiated form, a synthesis of empirical knowledge and practical techniques' (Parsons, 1964, p. 341). This view is clearly linked to the idea that humanity is primarily and uniquely defined by its ability to 'create and transmit culture' (Parsons, 1964, p. 341).

As primitive society gains a measure of control over its environment, the population and internal tensions increase. It becomes difficult to maintain social order and cultural traditions under a system that is essentially ascriptive and so, aided by the development of written language, a two-class system of social stratification emerges in which political and religious functions are centralized and become hereditary. Later on, with urbanization, a four-class system emerges, with two classes each in the rural and urban areas. Especially in the urban areas, a political-religious elite is formed. However, with government no longer based on ascription and kinship, new forms of legitimation are needed if the new social system is to survive, and these are obtained from the religious sector. In this way, increased differentiation is matched by the development of new institutions that function to maintain stability. Social stratification and legitimation are thus additional evolutionary universals, which serve to increase the adaptive capacity of the society and clear the way for further progress to a higher stage.

In so far as societies continue to evolve (and, for Parsons, evolution is not inevitable) there is further specialization, with renewed weakening of ascription. This is evident in the development of bureaucratic organization, an evolutionary universal linked by Parsons to another universal – the emergence of money and the money market. Like Weber, Parsons notes that bureaucratic authority resides in the office itself, rather than in the office holder and, again like Weber, he rates bureaucracy according to the criterion of efficiency; without it, large-scale organization would be impossible. Officials in bureaucracies are paid most easily in money which, for Parsons, is the great emancipator. It is

> the great mediator of the instrumental use of goods and services. Thus this universal 'emancipates' resources from such ascriptive bonds as demands to give kinship expectations priority, to be loyal in highly specific senses to certain political groups, or to submit the details of daily life to the specific imperatives of religious sects (Parsons, 1964, pp. 349-50).

For anyone even remotely familiar with Third World countries, bureaucracy need not necessarily be related to efficiency, and money, far from being an emancipator from ascriptive bonds may equally serve to reinforce them. This brings up the whole question of the relationships of Parsonian theory to empirical reality. However, it should be clear that what Parsons is doing is applying his pattern variables to social evolution, but in a far more specific and theoretical context than those who preceded him. He goes on to suggest that bureaucracy and the market system incorporate universalistic norms. True, they have existed in societies that can hardly be described as modern, but

> their crystallization into a coherent system represents a distinctive new step, which more than the industrial revolution

35

itself, ushered in the *modern* era of social evolution (Parsons, 1964, p. 351; author's emphasis).

In this way, modernity has come to be seen as primarily the result of new, more efficient social arrangements, with bureaucracy and the money market pre-eminent, and the industrial revolution itself is accorded a subsidiary position. The key to modernity is now universalistic norms. Indeed, Parsons goes further, when he states that it was English Common Law and its application to the English-speaking world that is 'the most important single hallmark of modern society' (1964, p. 353).

It should come as no surprise to discover that Parsons's final evolutionary universal is democratic association. In his view, this has four characteristics: the institutionalization of leaders in elective office, the franchise, procedural rules for voting and membership on a voluntary basis. In short, it is a political system markedly similar to the social democracies of Western Europe and North America, and one which is possible only after a universalistic normative order has been established.

In effect, Parsons presents us with a beguilingly simple outline of social evolution. Technology, kinship, language and religion are essential to any society. With the development of social stratification and cultural legitimation, there is a move away from primitiveness. Other evolutionary universals, notably bureaucratic organization, money and the money market, further increase the adaptive capacity of societies and may, in time, lead to that crucial breakthrough to modernity: a universalistic moral order. This, in turn, underpins the final universal, the modern political system.

In later works, (1966 and 1971) Parsons was more inclined to refer to specific stages of development, regarding social evolution as a process commencing at the primitive stage and leading, through an intermediate stage, to modernity, with every stage itself divided into three phases. In addition, he came to focus more on modern societies, which for him comprised highly differentiated systems, characterized above all by 'greater generalized adaptive capacity' (1971, p. 3). Such societies were seen to constitute a world system, linked by their common origin in Western Europe, especially seventeenth-century England, by a common cultural tradition based on Christianity and, indirectly, on the cultures of ancient Israel and Greece. It should be noted, too, that for Parsons modernity was extended beyond Europe 'only by colonization' (1971, p. 2). The only exception he allowed, and it was a partial one, was that of Japan, and even there, he points out, Western influence was marked. In the course of time, the United States took over the role of 'lead society' and there was a further break from the ascription inherent in European traditions of monarchy and aristocracy. The United States became more rational than other modern societies, in that the division of labour was no longer based on localized economies and, as immigration increased, citizenship and nationality ceased to be defined in ethnic terms. Instead, universalism was the dominant orientation, with ascription being further eroded by the introduction of egalitarianism in education. Parsons went on to claim that

American society has gone farther than any comparable large-scale society in its dissociation from the older ascriptive inequalities and the institutionalization of a basically egalitarian pattern (1971, p. 114).

In all of this, the main processes of social change are differentiation, adaptive upgrading (which seems to mean a more efficient use of resources), the inclusion of new units, structures and mechanisms in the normative order and, finally, the generalization of values. Although Parsons applies the pattern variables less simplistically than Hoselitz, it is evidently his view that modernization entails a movement from ascription to achievement, from particularism to universalism, and from diffuseness to specificity.

At this point, it is necessary to make two qualifications. First, Parsons does not suggest that all societies must pass through the same stages. Herein lies the importance of diffusion. One must

distinguish the first occurrence of a social innovation from its subsequent diffusion. The latter can occur without the whole set of prerequisite societal conditions necessary for the former (Parsons, 1964, p. 353).

Put in plain English, this means that it is easier to pass on the message than to originate it. How a society acquires an evolutionary universal does not greatly matter, as long as it is acquired.

Secondly, social evolution is not inevitable. Societies which fail to develop new universals need not become extinct; instead, they may remain in special 'niches', in a symbiotic relationship with more developed societies. 'They are not, by and large, major threats to the continued existence of the evolutionary higher systems' (Parson, 1964, p. 341). Elsewhere, Parsons suggests that

> The primitive societies studied by anthropologists are of this type. Quite clearly, we must postulate that their characteristics significantly approximate those of our own actual pre-historical antecedents, (1966, p. 110).

To put it somewhat mildly, the Parsonian variant of neo-evolutionism is not without its problems. First, it is not at all clear why we should assume that the characteristics of existing small-scale societies are akin to the social structures of the prehistoric West, and the chances of the relevant technical procedures being developed to make the comparison are remote. In any case, Parsons paid little attention to contemporary, non-industrialized societies, favouring (he claims) a more historical approach. The avowed focus does not exempt him from the charge of a-historicism.

Secondly, Parsons follows Weber in the use of historical material in forming ideal types, but although he is concerned with developmental sequences, it might be argued that he ignored Weber's warning against confusing ideal types and reality (Weber, 1949, p. 101). Undoubtedly, he attempts to relate his evolutionary stages to actual societies, past and present. Like Durkheim, for instance, he regards Australian aboriginal society as primitive and, at the other end of the evolutionary scale, Western Europe, the USA, the Soviet Union and Japan are considered modern. However, there is an obvious ethnocentricism in the thinly disguised portrayal of the United States as the most 'modern' of all societies, and his characterization of his own society as espousing universalism and egalitarianism leaves much to be desired. At the time he was writing, the United States was periodically wracked by race riots, a violent protest against ascription, if ever there was one, and it was also heavily involved in the Vietnam war. As Gouldner remarks of Parsons, in a slightly different context, the overwhelming impression in his writing is 'one of self-congratulatory celebration' (Gouldner, 1971, p. 48).

Thirdly, as Hoogvelt points out, Parsons presents us with 'a *sequential* order of structural types' (1976, p. 50; author's emphasis), that nevertheless 'suggests quite deliberately a *historical* sequel which is never properly backed up be historical research' (1976, p. 51 author's emphasis). In these circumstances, there is no reason to suppose that the evolutionary pattern described by Parsons would have occurred, if 'external penetration' (Hoogvelt, 1976, p. 65) had not affected the Third World. In fact, it is difficult to escape the conclusion that the process Parsons puts forward owes more to his evaluation of the United States and its social institutions than to an historical understanding of development. Indeed, it is quite remarkable how little Parsons had to say on the 'modernization' of existing societies. In the article and the two books to which I have referred, he allocates a total of two paragraphs to the subject (1971, p. 137). First, he suggests that 'the trend toward modernization has now become world-wide. In particular, the elites of most nonmodern societies accept crucial aspects of the values of modernity' (1971, p. 137). Secondly, he argues that a Third World bloc might emerge as a stabilizing factor in international politics and as an agent for modernization and, finally, he speculates that Japan could become an important 'model' for 'modernizing' societies. These passing references, for that is all they are, along with the idealization of the North American experience, do not add up to a convincing basis for the sociology of development.

Fourthly, in Parsons, as with the forerunners who adapted some of his ideas, there is little recognition of the magnitude of the colonial experience. When a reference does occur, colonialism is regarded as a positive influence in the development of modernity. In addition, there is no indication that the colonized peoples made any significant contribution to the development of the First World. As will be clear in the following chapter, a focus on such issues is at the centre of the neo-Marxist critique of modernization theory. What Parsons does do, more comprehensively than his predecessors, is to place the role of values, the entire normative order, at the centre of the development stage. Despite the importance of other evolutionary universals, it is universalism per se, and its institutional manifestations in the legal and political systems, enshrined in the Judaeo-Christian tradition, which comes to be seen as the hallmark of modernity and which should be diffused from the West to the Third World.

Finally, a different problem arises with the notion of evolution. Parsons and his collaborators reintroduced this somewhat discredited idea and placed it firmly at the centre of the study of social change. Evolution meant progress, and progress was achieved by becoming more like Western Europe and the United States. Third World societies could either remain in 'niches', caught up in some kind of time warp, or join the general trend by adopting, through diffusion, especially via their elites, the cultural characteristics of the advanced societies. It is easy to reject the ethnocentricism inherent in this approach; however, if we (as sociologists, as developers, or as those about to be developed) believe that development is in any way 'progressive', and also reject the United States as the 'lead society', we must put something else in its place. In brief, if there is an evolutionary process, where is it leading?

For Levy, who had already utilized the Parsonian pattern variables in his earlier work, (1952a and 1952b), modernization was defined as a continuum, according to the degree to which inanimate power and tools were developed (1966, p. 35). In this sense, it might be argued that, for him, the key element in evolution was technological progress, and the process of evolution simply led to increased human control of the physical environment. Nevertheless, the social structural concomitants of this process are described in terms virtually identical to those employed by Parsons. Levy distinguished between 'relatively modernized' and 'relatively nonmodernized' societies, and considered the former to be high on specialization, universalism, centralization, rationality and functional specificity, possessing bureaucratic organization, a highly generalized medium of exchange and developed markets. As we would expect, 'relatively nonmodernized' societies evidenced the very opposite of these characteristics. For Levy, more than Parsons, modernization was inevitable, and would have occurred even without imperialism, necessarily subverting traditional social structures, aspects of which he regarded as incompatible with modernization. However,

Levy was well aware of the disruptive elements in modernization: with an increase in specialization and interdependence social structures come under attack, none more so than the family, which approximates increasingly to the nuclear family common throughout Western Europe and North America. Most of all, with modernization comes instability:

> The more highly modernized the society concerned, the more involved in the process of modernization, the greater is the implication of instability emanating from any social context for its members... Vulnerability inheres in any contact the members of such societies have with those of relatively modernized societies. Any such contacts increase interdependence (Levy, 1966, pp. 789-90).

Certainly, this focus on instability as a key element in modernization distinguishes Levy from Parsons, who never was one to emphasize subversion, instability and the breakdown of social control in social systems. In addition, Levy's perception of modernity and nonmodernity as relative, rather than absolute states, is a welcome relief from Parsons's idealization of the United States. However, in the end Levy's evolutionary path is as unilinear, as ethnocentric, and even more relentless than that of Parsons, with identical social structural and cultural ramifications. The path to relative modernity may be more fraught, but is is undoubtedly one in which increased Westernization continues to be the goal.

## Variants of Modernization Theory

It is now common, especially among adherents of underdevelopment theory, to depict modernization theory as more or less coterminous with Parsonian neo-evolutionism. Undoubtedly, at the level of metatheory, or 'grand theory', Parsons was supreme. He had been instrumental in providing the structural functionalist base on which early modernization studies had leaned so heavily, and then he threw his weight behind the renewed emphasis on evolution. At a slightly less abstract level, such structural functionalists as Smelser (1969) and Eisenstadt (1964, 1966 and 1968) had produced models that were intended to be applied in the study of Third World social change. Generally, the concepts used, and the key criteria of modernization, were derived from earlier generalizations of sociologists, and this was also true for the concept of evolution. In Eisenstadt (1970), there is a comprehensive summary of neo-evolutionist modernization theory at that time: societies are treated as structural functional wholes, made up of institutions and individuals in structural positions. As such, they are adaptive systems, and progress from one evolutionary stage to another is indicated by increased differentiation and interdependence, not only within the system but within the international context. In particular, there is a need for 'special "entrepreneurs" or an elite able to offer solutions to the new range of problems' (Eisenstadt, 1970, p. 19), and the stronger the elite the greater the progress. Of course, increased social differentiation brings its own complications: new social groups are prone to conflict and need to be controlled and integrated. The answers to this problem – and the ensuing institutional structures – will vary because of differences in the starting points of modernizing societies, and because a variety of approaches will be adopted by modernizing elites.

At a more empirical level, sociologists, as well as other social scientists, were interested in the role of individual change agents, and in the twin processes of innovation and diffusion. Generally speaking, it was assumed that innovation occurred in 'modern' societies and was then diffused into 'traditional' societies. Technological change was not totally ignored, but in the exchange culture – especially 'modern' norms and values – was regarded as a key factor in social change. In addition, more specific social institutions were not neglected and it became fashionable to refer to the modernization of this, that, or the other; education, religion, law, administration, technology, industry, agriculture, the city, communications, mankind itself, could and should be modernized, for therein lay the secret of economic growth, and the good news was broadcast throughout the Third World by the mass media, including the Voice of America (Weiner, 1966). True, there was a chicken and egg problem: it was never clear whether changes in values preceded economic change or vice versa. Nevertheless, it was generally agreed that in development, normally regarded as economic growth, cultural change was crucial.

Neo-evolutionism may have been dominant at the end of the 1960s, but even among modernization theorists there were voices of dissent, and some of these had been heard even before Frank's onslaught on modernization theory was published in English (1969). It was not universally agreed, for example, that tradition and modernity were incompatible. Singer (1966) insisted that religions other than Christian protestantism were able to facilitate industrial development, and that Asian societies, far from being static, were able to adjust their religious institutions to the demands of modernization. He echoed Srinivas (1962) in pointing to the links between Sanskritization, where lower castes increasingly emulate the upper castes, and Westernization in India, and suggested that Hinduism was able to absorb rather than obstruct the processes of modernization.

From a very different perspective, M.G. Smith argued that it was often the case that allegedly opposing pattern variables would co-exist in a single society, and that it was simply reductionist to focus on values and normative consensus. He developed the notion of 'plural society' (cf. Smith, 1965), with specific reference to the Caribbean, a region transformed economically and ethnically by slavery and colonialism. As a result, there was no common value system; instead, disparate strata which, however coherent internally, were linked primarily through economic necessity and whose orderly relations were preserved through the exercise of force by a minority over the majority. Stratification 'cannot be adequately studied in terms of underlying value orientations; it represents an order interdependent with the political order based on certain concrete structural principles' (Smith, 1966, p. 174). The notion of plural society was to be considerably modified, and later Smith was to argue that whilst forms of social association and cultural institutions might vary across strata without political and legal inequalities, an unequal access to the public domain would lead to different cultures and forms of social organization. It thus becomes possible to refer to structural, social and cultural pluralism, where the last two can exist, or co-exist, without entailing structural pluralism but where, too, structural pluralism must logically entail social pluralism and where both structural and social pluralism involve differences in culture. In Smithian terms, 'structural and social pluralism both assume and express cultural pluralism, but in different forms and with differing intensities' (Smith, 1974, p. 335). For Smith, what is crucial is to understand the structural principles whereby groups and individuals are incorporated into societies. Such principles are, at base, political. His structuralism, developed in studying a part of the Third World that has variously been described as modernizing or underdeveloped, poses a direct, albeit little known, challenge to Parsonian consensus theory. The point to note here is that for Smith, as for others, the pattern variables so popular among modernization theorists were less than helpful in understanding social change in the Third World: to emphasize role orientation was to focus on the derivative. A more realistic focus would be on the structural principles that form the basis of social and economic association. In the end, political power is the key.

One of the strongest objections to the standard polarization of tradition and modernity, and, indeed, to the neo-evolutionist perspective in modernization theory, came from Bendix, a political sociologist much concerned with the development of 'new nations'. At the theoretical level, Bendix is a Weberian, interested in the nature of political power and authority, and in using ideal type constructs to compare social phenomena in different societies. Like Weber, Bendix uses ideal types to focus on specific empirical contexts, and combines them with a wide-ranging historical analysis.

First, Bendix argues that the 'disjunctive characterization of "tradition" and "universalism" exaggerates and simplifies the evidence' (1967, p. 314). Such labelling serves to confuse the abstract nature of ideal types with empirical reality and runs the risk of projecting Western experience on to the Third World as a mono-causal, uniform and inevitable process. In short, it is an example of 'misplaced evolutionism'.

Secondly, it is not the case that tradition and modernity are exclusive characteristics of self-regulating systems; rather, elements of tradition will be found in modern societies, and allegedly 'modern' characteristics will be operating in 'traditional' societies. In any case, it is simply inaccurate to regard 'new nations' as closed, self-regulating systems. As Bendix remarks, since revolutions in England and France – and even then – 'every subsequent process of modernization has combined intrinsic changes with external stimuli' (1967, p. 326). Communication, for example, is international, and to understand how modernization occurs we must examine the ways in which ideas are diffused across national boundaries. Intellectuals and government officials, in particular, are subject to influences from outside:

> The facts are that intellectuals have played a major role in helping to transform the social structure of backward societies and have done so more often than not in reference to prior economic and political developments abroad. Likewise, government officials have played a major role in the development of economic resources, or have supported and implemented an institutional framework in which such a development became easier. (Bendix, 1967, p. 327).

Bendix goes on to suggest that once the process of modernization has commenced, it has ramifications outside the 'lead' society in which it occurred, and 'follower' societies will develop. As a consequence, the overall national and international context is changed: 'Once industrialization has occurred anywhere, this fact alone alters the international environment of other societies. There is a sense in which it is true to say that because of timing and sequence industrialization cannot occur in the same way twice' (Bendix, 1967, p. 328).

Such a view is clearly at odds with neo-evolutionist and structural functionalist perspectives which stress the inevitability and unilinear nature of modernization. In addition, Bendix suggests that some aspects of modernity, for example, widespread literacy, increased medical provisions and extensions of the franchise, may be introduced without achieving full 'modernity', as evidenced in the current 'lead' society. Indeed, 'follower' societies may instigate these changes in the hope that they will provide 'short cuts' to modernity, and Bendix notes that they may be easier to introduce than advanced, capital-intensive technology. In all of this, Bendix regards the role of Third World governments as a key factor and one which, by and large, has been ignored by evolutionists, who have tended to see government as epiphenomenal:

> The view that government is an integral part of the social structure, but may have the capacity of altering it significantly, is not in the mainstream of social theory... Yet in studies of the modernization of complex societies it is more useful

to consider social structure and government, or society and the state, as interdependent, but also relatively autonomous, spheres of thought and action (Bendix, 1967, p. 333).

Bendix's concern with internal social structures, and their links with the wider social context, is revealed in his empirical study of modernization in Japan, which he quite clearly relates to Weber's study of the Protestant Ethic. His main focus is on the role of the Samurai, who were instrumental in transforming Japanese society in the late nineteenth century. Over two centuries, they had ceased to be rural landowners and militants and had become, instead, urban retainers, nevertheless retaining an ideological commitment to self-discipline, action and militancy. When Japan was faced with a threat from the USA, and undergoing the national trauma of military involvement, occupation and international struggle, it was forced to redefine its national goals, and it was through the Samurai and their apparently outdated values that the threat was met. The old virtues, and the transformed class, became the key to the new order. In essence, the Samurai were the 'functional equivalents' of the Puritans:

> There is no need to examine the manifest dissimilarities between the English Reformation and the Japanese response to the Western challenge. In both instances motivation was intensified along established lines, apparently because the context stimulated a heightened concern with the supreme value of personal salvation or national integrity, respectively. The two cases suggest that the cultural-educational preconditions of economic development can be understood more clearly if the internal structure of a society is analysed in relation to its political structure and international setting (Bendix, 1966, p. 278).

It is not that Bendix rejects all established modernization theory. He accepts Smelser's depiction of the effects of economic development on social structures, that is, changes from simple to complex technology, subsistence farming to cash crops, animal and human power to industrialization, and increased urbanization. Further, he acknowledges that structural functionalism may be useful in analysing Third World social change but opposes the closed-system approach, and also recognizes that development in the Third World is neither inevitable nor unilinear. In addition, he warns against 'the fallacy of the golden age' in the study of Western European development, and the 'fallacy of retrospective determinism' in the attempt to impose a uniform pattern of development on all nations. Above all, perhaps, he directs us away from the logic of system coherence and neo-evolutionism towards more empirical examinations of social structures:

> The point is that countries which come late to the process of development possess social structures which must be understood in their own terms rather than merely as 'transitional stages' to the type of industrialized society exemplified by the English or, better still, the American case (Bendix, 1964, p. 213).

In Bendix, we have a view of different patterns of development where 'new nations', in an international context, compete to be 'leader' and 'follower' societies, and where the diffusion of ideas and technology criss-crosses national boundaries. In all of this, internal social and political structures, class alignments and values, are clearly relevant, and due importance is given to the role of intellectuals and the state, albeit subject to external influences and constraints. And these ideas are actually applied in the empirical and historical study of social change in specific societies, which itself distinguishes the work of Bendix from that of Parsons. It might be argued that power and international economic structures figure but little in Bendix, but the fact remains that he provides a powerful critique of Parsonian neo-evolutionism and structural functionalism from within the 'paradigm' (if that is what it is) of modernization theory.

An even wider ranging critique of neo-evolutionist theory can be found in Barrington Moore's detailed study of the *Social Origins of Dictatorship and Democracy* (1967). His main thesis is that there are three routes from pre-industrial to modern society: 'bourgeois' revolutions, as in England and the United States, fascist revolutions 'from above', as in Japan and Germany, and Communist revolutions 'from below', as seen in Russia and China. In analysing how these revolutions occurred, Barrington Moore focuses especially on the inter-linkages of social classes, most notably those between the landed upper classes and the peasantry, and he does so in a highly empirical, historical survey in which he charts these main routes to the modern world. In addition, he attempts to show why India, at the time he was writing, had been unable to achieve the status of an industrial society.

Critics of Barrington Moore have argued that his work is too long, too detailed, unclear, or that much of his empirical findings are open to other interpretations. (cf. Ness *et al*, 1967). However, for present purposes these are secondary issues. What is more relevant, perhaps, is that he 'never articulates, in general terms, the set of structural conditions which ought to bear the ultimate burden of interpretation' (Poggi, 1968, p. 217), and that he does not relate his approach to that of other sociologists, especially Bendix (Poggi, 1968, p. 217). Nevertheless, although Barrington Moore may best be regarded as a modernization theorist who has much in common with Bendix, there are also elements of underdevelopment theory in his work, which may be said to contain elements of both perspectives. The links with modernization theory are numerous. First, he stresses that innovation at the political level is a key factor in modern, 'leader' states. This is not intended to be a general statement about all societies at all times, rather a recognition that, at different historical periods, specific societies have undergone structural changes which not only have led to considerable economic advances but also have made them models for other societies to follow. Below the level of political leadership, too, he is cognisant of the importance of entrepreneurial activity and innovative technological change; nevertheless, he warns us against too heavy an emphasis on such factors, pointing out that what is important is the overall social structure within which entrepreneurs and innovators operate. Clearly, these are issues familiar to modernization theorists.

Secondly, even though Barrington Moore is personally convinced that Western technology is destined to spread throughout the world (cf. p. 378), his main thesis makes it quite clear that there are different routes to modernity. He is no unilinear theorist. In addition, modern societies need be neither capitalist nor democratic. We can have 'nondemocratic and even antidemocratic modernization' (p. 159). Further, it is a mistake to regard changes that have occurred in some societies as inevitable for others. In nineteenth-century England, a relatively peaceful transition to industrialization was founded upon more violent seventeenth and eighteenth centuries, but this connection was neither necessary nor inevitable and to assert otherwise 'is to justify the present by the past with an argument that is impossible to prove' (p. 29). In similar vein, he asserts that neither the French Revolution nor the later liberal democracy in France were inevitable (p. 108), and that the stagnation of Indian development was not bound to happen:

> To speak of a vicious circle may carry the implication that the situation was hopeless. This is not so. As historical experience in other recently industrialized countries shows, a policy exists which can break the circle. In their broad essentials, the problem and the answer are very simple. They amount to using a combination of economic incentives and political compulsion to induce the people on the land to improve productivity and at the same time taking a substantial part of the surplus so generated to construct an industrial society. Behind this problem there stands a political one, whether or not a class of people has arisen in the society with the capacity and ruthlessness to force through the changes (Moore, 1967, p. 385-6).

Thirdly, as this quotation indicates, Moore (like Bendix) gives considerable importance to the political sphere. At times, for example, when the British remained in India after establishing economic control, this seems to take precedence over economic factors. At other times, he stresses the importance of strong political leadership, as in the cases of Gandhi and Nehru, and he also accepts that one cannot ignore the role of culture. Nevertheless, he is insistent that cultural variables alone cannot explain India's failure to develop. Values must always be related to the structural context in which they occur and by which they are moulded. Here, he is quite specific in opposing the Parsonian conception of normative consensus, emphasizing the fact that 'social inertia' cannot be assumed. Social order should not be taken for granted. What all of this should indicate is that although Barrington Moore recognizes the importance of economic causes, his social structural approach has no place for mono-causal explanations: culture, politics, individual leadership, and economic interests all have their parts to play, but they play different roles in different societies at different times. In such an analysis, with so much empirical data, it is perhaps inevitable that there will be inconsistencies. Moore recognizes that the Indian caste system has an economic base but this does not prevent him from reverting to a more conventional analysis using the 'traditional' and 'modern' dichotomy:

> At a deeper level of causation the Mutiny shows how the intrusion of the West, with its stress on commerce and industry, its secular and scientific attitude towards the physical world, its emphasis on demonstrable competence in a job rather than on inherited status, posed a fundamental threat to Indian society. Together and separately, these features were incompatible with an agrarian civilization organized around caste and its religious sanctions (Moore, 1967, p. 350).

For much of the time, then, Barrington Moore uses concepts which are to be found in the work of other modernization theorists, albeit in such a way as to cast doubt on their overall applicability. He does not even oppose the concept of evolution, simply remarking that 'no country goes through all the stages, but merely carries the development a certain distance within the framework of its own situation and institutions' (1967, p. 427). Yet it should be evident that he has more in common with Bendix than with Parsons, a similarity that perhaps arises from their mutual concern with empirical data. At the same time, there is a sense in which he pre-dates underdevelopment theory or, at least, its popularization in the English-speaking world. He is quite explicit that change occurs in a world context, and not merely in economic structures. The success of the French Revolution ended hopes of rapid reform in England, as peaceful democratic revolution in that country required 'acceptable regimes in Europe' (1967, p. 31). In a different context, Japanese military success and the later occupation of China were 'decisive' in bringing about the victory of the Chinese communists. Indeed, Japan itself was prompted to modernize by the threat from the West, a modernization brought about, among other reasons, by a powerful modernizing elite. If we switch to yet another society, he makes it quite clear that the American Civil War was very much the scenario of an interaction among three sub-systems: the South, the West and the

North-east, with the colonial power also much involved. Here, if it were needed, is a reminder that revolutions in one society are crucially influenced by the nature of the links that society has with others, in a world social and economic system, where not only present linkages are important but also where the history of one society, a 'leader', may be of crucial importance to the later development of another.

It should be evident that the concept of 'world system' is not foreign to Barrington Moore, even if he did not elaborate it in the single-minded manner of Frank. However, it should also be noted that in Moore's work there is, already, a partial critique of some of the main tenets of underdevelopment theory, at least in their crudest forms. He is quite prepared to cast doubt on a simplistic interpretation of Chinese or Indian underdevelopment:

> Marxists make too much of the way Western imperialists stifled industrial development in China. (Nationalists in India also use this convenient scapegoat.) None of this could have happened without prior stifling by purely domestic forces (Moore, 1967, p. 177).

In the same manner, he warns us against the danger of 'reading off' economic from political power: 'Men who hold power do not necessarily exercise it simply in the interests of the class from which they arise, especially in changing situations' (p. 37).

The political sphere must be studied in its own right. Indeed, political mechanisms may be crucial in determining how the economic surplus was extracted in France and England (pp. 63-4) and in India (p. 355), where Barrington Moore regards the failure of the Indian government to collect and utilize the surplus as a key feature in India's 'backwardness'.

At a somewhat different level, he is concerned with the effects of modernization on the peasantry. For the peasant, modernization involves an increase in market relationships and production for the market, with a corresponding decline in subsistence production, all of which are best achieved in an overall context of peace and stability, ensured by a strong central government. However, when the peasantry is exploited by central government and lacks links with the landed upper classes, and is also denied the opportunity to participate in commercial agriculture, peasant rebellion is a distinct possibility, especially if social solidarity among the peasantry is high. In such circumstances, peasant unrest may become a rebellion or even a revolution, always provided that leadership is available from outside the peasantry. 'By themselves, the peasants have never been able to accomplish a revolution' (Barrington Moore, 1967, p. 479). For Barrington Moore, all modernization, irrespective of the route taken, involves the eradication of the peasantry: 'At bottom, all forms of industrialization so far have been revolutions from above, the work of a ruthless minority' (p. 508).

It should be evident that Barrington Moore is not a modernization theorist in the Parsonian mould. He was as concerned as Parsons with the development of modernity and did at least pay passing lip service to the notion of evolution. However, much of his criticism of established modernization theory is implicit and, like Bendix, he sets out to chart the routes taken by specific and contrasting societies towards modernity. Like Bendix, too, he notes the importance of external linkages, both economic and political, on the operation of internal, domestic social structures, and in his analysis of the causes of modernization he takes a multi-causal perspective, arguing that at various times, economic, political, social and cultural factors all have their parts to play. Finally, in his focus on the peasantry, he attempts to demonstrate the effects that the processes of modernization have upon peasants as a class, and suggests that, in the end, irrespective of the route followed to modernization, it is the peasantry that pays the cost.

It is noticeable that, with the partial exception of Barrington Moore, few modernization theorists have examined the ways in which modernity impinges on everyday life. This criticism, however, cannot be levelled at Berger and his associates who, developing an earlier work (Berger and Luckmann, 1967), set out to describe the effect of modernization on the consciousness of ordinary people. It is essential to note that Berger and Luckmann emphasized that human society can be regarded as both objectively experienced and individually created. Combining Durkheim and Weber, they focus on the mechanisms by which actors internalize the world 'out there' and yet recreate and change the social world into which they are born. Reality is socially constructed and human agency is responsible. In a sense, it is at the level of human consciousness that objective and subjective reality merge, irrespective of the level of 'development' in a society. The process is the same whether the society is 'modern' or 'modernizing'.

Applying the phenomenological perspective derived from Berger and Luckmann, Berger and his associates view modernization as

> the institutional concomitants of technologically induced economic growth. This means that there is no such thing as a 'modern society' plain and simple; there are only societies more or less advanced in a continuum of modernization.
>
> Modernization, then, consists of the growth and diffusion of a set of institutions rooted in the transformation of the economy by means of technology (Berger *et al.* 1974, p. 15).

In this technologically induced process of social change, some institutions are regarded as more important than others. Those connected with the economy or with the apparatus of the modern state, such as bureaucracy, are accorded special importance. They are 'primary carriers' of modernization. In addition, there are other institutional processes that induce modernization, referred to as 'secondary carriers'.

The authors are particularly concerned with the effects of technological change on consciousness, on the ways in which individuals perceive their world and their position in it. In this sense, they continue the focus in modernization theory on values and the role of culture. However, rather than promote consciousness to the level of a 'prime mover', or repeat social psychological studies of values, they utilize the phenomenological perspective of Berger and Luckmann (1967), and suggest that consciousness of everyday life is the 'web of meanings' shared with others, the totality of which 'makes up a particular social life-world' (Berger *et al.*, 1974, p. 18).

Technology and bureaucracy impose a Weberian kind of rationality on production and on all who participate in it. However, their influence does not stop at the factory gate or the office door; it permeates other spheres of social life where problems can be addressed and solved and where self-identity is questioned. Other institutions, for example, education and the mass media, act as 'secondary carriers', thus reinforcing the 'modern' perspective which involves nothing less than the compartmentalization of social life.

In the face of such pressures, the world can no longer be taken for granted. There is now a 'pluralization of life-worlds'. Decisions must be made according to different criteria, and individuals now have to choose from competing values, ideologies and legitimators. In short, they experience anomie, and traditional religion and traditional authorities can no longer provide the desired security:

> The final consequence of all this can be put very simply (though the simplicity is deceptive): *modern man has suffered from a deepening condition of homelessness* (Berger *et al.*, 1974, p. 77; authors' emphasis).

In effect, what Berger and his colleagues are doing is elaborating on the work of Durkheim and Weber. Certain consequences of modernization are regarded as inevitable, even though they will be differentially experienced throughout the Third World and within any Third World society. Ultimately, such effects are different in degree rather than in kind. To use the authors' somewhat inelegant jargon, rationality, componentiality, multi-relationality, makeability, plurality and progressivity are intrinsic to technological production, and all are generalizable to non-economic spheres of activity. Through the influence of bureaucratic organization, society itself comes to be seen as an objective reality, which can be acted upon and changed, albeit within bureaucratically defined areas of influence. Indeed, all social life comes to be divided into public and private sectors – the result of a prevalence of bureaucratic thinking.

Modernization, diffused from the West, tends to lead to new standards of comparison. The poor discover their own poverty, and increase their awareness of their position by comparing themselves with the rich. Dissatisfaction may be directed at the West, at their own governments, or both, and for a time nationalism may cushion the discrepancy. However, there is also likely to be increased support for radical political movements. Indeed, in such a situation, socialism has obvious advantages. 'If modernization can be described as a spreading condition of homelessness, then socialism can be understood as the promise of a new home' (Berger *et al.*, 1974, p. 124). Of course, the extent to which the promise is fulfilled will vary, and elsewhere (like Barrington Moore) Berger concludes that there are enormous costs in both socialist and capitalist development strategies (Berger, 1977).

Attempts may be made to counter the modernization process. 'Modernization may be *encapsulated*, contained in a kind of enclave, around which the traditional patterns of life go on substantially as before' (Berger *et al.*, 1974, p. 139; authors' emphasis). Compromises will be made. New ideologies may develop, ranging in ethos from outright welcome to direct opposition. And yet even opposition to modernization will be tinged, or tainted, with modernity. As in Weber's description of the growth of rationality in the modern world (1948, p. 55), such opposition runs counter to the spirit of the age.

As I have already suggested, the work of Berger and his colleagues can be linked to that of Durkheim who emphasized the increasing complexity of modern life under an all-embracing division of labour, and to Weber, whose views on the spread of rationality and bureaucracy are, in my view, essentially evolutionist. Like Durkheim and Weber, too, Berger and his colleagues regard modernization as a process which is, by and large, identical to Western development. According to one critic their ethnocentricism extends to a myopic perspective even of North American society (Stanton, 1975, p. 37), and, rightly, Stanton also criticizes the unnecessary proliferation of terms as a symptom 'of the malady *categorism*. This is the tendency to suppose that thinking up a category within which to fit a phenomenon is the same as understanding the phenomenon' (1975, p. 38; emphasis in the original).

Stanton also suggests that Berger and his co-authors fail to relate their major units of analysis to one another, to a social order, and to history, and that implicit in their approach is the primacy of the individual and individual consciousness, with a corresponding reluctance to focus on social groups and social conflict. There is foundation for both these criticisms. However, it must also be said that they firmly locate their work in the phenomenological perspective developed by Berger and Luckmann, itself derived from the concerns of some of the classical sociologists, including Durkheim and Weber. In addition, it might be argued that such notions as shared realities, a pluralization of life worlds, symbolic universes and sub-universes of meaning necessarily refer as much to group consciousness as to that of the individual. By its nature, from their perspective, consciousness is, by definition, shared. It is indeed the case that we are not provided with a class analysis, but the authors never set out to give us one. Instead, what they are setting out to demonstrate is that the process of modernization, derived from the transformation of the economy, is reflected in the total range of social institutions in any society. In short, the shared experience of social life is itself traumatized and transformed as a result of this process. What is perhaps more important is that it is doubtful if they have really applied their phenomenological perspective consistently to the Third World. Instead of investigating the dialectical relationship between consciousness and technology, the former somehow becomes a derivative of the latter. The fault is compounded if one actually considers that consciousness and culture, however defined, should be investigated in their own right.

In some respects, the concerns of Berger and his colleagues can be related to those of Parsons and other modernization theorists. There is a focus on culture, on diffusion, on increased differentiation, and a general implication that Westernization and modernization are synonymous. However, their work is a far cry from the search for a 'mobile personality' and the individual attributes of 'modern man'. Rather, there is a deeper awareness that economic and technological change can, and often do, transform the life of a people and, at a less abstract level, their idea that change often comes in 'packages' is both interesting and valid. On reflection, it is evident that the introduction of modern methods of production will have far-reaching effects. It is not just an economic change: 'reality is redefined and reclassified in almost every sector of social life' (Berger *et al.*, 1974, p. 131). This theoretical approach is given some empirical validity when one looks, for example, at China and the concern on the part of the authorities that economic and technological changes do not lead to wholesale changes in Chinese culture. True, it is an empirical question just how much of the package any one society has to accept – and, indeed, what is in the package – but the idea that when you accept economic advance (and not just of a capitalist type) you are going to have to make concessions elsewhere, seems to me to be both useful and evident. All of this may merely be a re-working of the traditional-modern dichotomy, but it is no less relevant for that.

Although Berger and his colleagues escaped the initial on-slaught on modernization theory, they might be accused by underdevelopment theorists of neglecting the importance of both economic and colonial experience. By now, this kind of criticism is standard. However, they undoubtedly provide an interesting and sophisticated development of modernization theory, which links them not only with such 'classical' sociologists as Durkheim and Weber but also with the neo-evolutionist, diffusionist per-spectives taken by Parsons and his supporters. In addition, they can hardly be accused of ignoring economic factors, given that it is economic growth and technological change which are, in effect, the prime movers of social and cultural change, including changes in the consciousness of those who are in the process of being developed and of developing themselves.

## *Summary*

The neo-evolutionism of Parsons and his followers, emerging as it did in the mid-1960s, added a degree of theoretical sophistication to the sociology of development and, in a sense, justifies the sepa-ration of this chapter from the preceding one. It is an indication of the importance of Parsons, who dominated sociological thought for the two decades that followed the Second World War, that with a shift in his thinking there was a corresponding movement in the focus of sociology as a whole. However, the break between the two chapters may also be considered somewhat arbitrary, the result more of convenience and chronology than of epistemology. Neo-evolutionism was a revival of classical evolutionism, and its non-Marxist critics also drew on previous intellectual traditions, especially Max Weber. In the following chapters, too, it will be shown that the intellectual debt to the past of underdevelopment theorists, the neo-Marxists, is also considerable.

By now, it should be evident that by the end of the 1960s, there was no single modernization 'theory'. Instead, a wide variety of approaches were subsumed under the term, ranging from the psychological to the metatheoretical, along with a considerable body of empirical inquiry. As one might expect, and as Figure 1 indicates, the intellectual origins of these perspectives are similarly diffuse. It is possible to note some familiar themes and assumptions, but it must be remembered that they are not shared equally by all members of the so-called school, even though it has become fashionable to criticize modernization ttheory as a whole (Bernstein, 1971 and 1979; Tipps, 1973; Higgott, 1978).

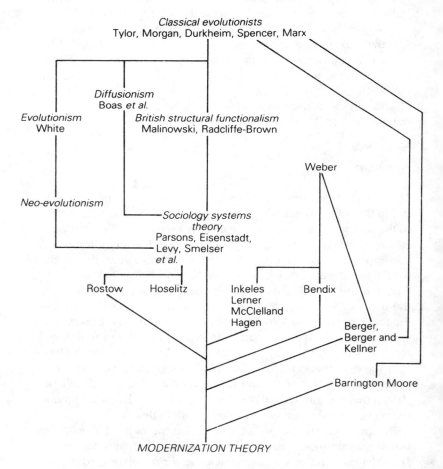

**Figure 1** The Development of Modernization Theory

First, the unit on which many modernization theorists focus is the nation-state. In fact, there is nothing sacrosanct about this unit of analysis in structural-functionalist methodology, which simply states that once the 'whole' had been decided upon, its constituent parts should be examined within that context. There is no reason why the focus should not be on some smaller, pre-defined unit, for example, a village, and social anthropologists have traditionally specialized in such units. By the same token, Parsons himself referred to the system of modern societies (which gives him something in common with the 'world system' approach in underdevelopment theory). However, the fact that many countries obtained political independence in the period following the Second World War encouraged social scientists to examine them as 'wholes', and politically, too, such projects coincided with the interests of grant-awarding governments who were much concerned with the political stability and ideological orientation of the new states. This political concern with social order was also reflected in structural functionalism, which viewed societies as self-regulating systems, emphasized equilibrium, and did not normally lead to a consideration of social conflict.

Secondly, much of modernization theory is implicitly or explicitly evolutionary, which is not to say that all evolutionists are modernization theorists. However, there does appear to be some kind of 'fit' between structural functionalist and evolutionist perspectives. Talk of 'adaptive capacity', for example, as the principle of system maintenance suggests a movement from one point, or stage, to another, and the concern with stages of development can be traced back to the classical evolutionists. Even in the absence of stages, it is necessary to decide the criteria of movement: increased social differentiation and institutional complexity, along with the growth of formal rationality and industrialization, are common indices. Indeed, as Tipps points out, both rationality and industrialization have been used as 'critical variables' in theories that equate modernization with one kind of social change (Tipps, 1973, p. 203). He goes on to suggest that most modernization theory is 'dichotomous' (or, in Frank's term, 'ideal typical') in that its exponents conceptualize change from one polar type to another. Less abstractly, in attempting to describe the change to modernity, some writers have recommended other indices, for example, literacy, the spread of mass media, urbanization, or the existence of a 'democratic' – that is, electoral – political system. In short, there is a tendency among modernization theorists to see the end point of evolution of underdeveloped societies as the Western present, or some aspect of it.

Thirdly, modernization theory tends to postulate the idea of 'dual societies'. This view, also shared by some economists and geographers, arises from the idea that underdeveloped societies either repeat the history of the industrialized West or remain underdeveloped. As industrial enclaves arise, or are implanted, within traditional societies, modern and traditional sectors co-exist, albeit not without tension. Gradually, the influence of the modern sector, the 'growth pole', radiates until the rural, traditional environment is transformed, economically, politically and socially.

Despite the obvious importance of industrial development in the process of social change, which is taken for granted by many modernization theorists, most of them focus on social and cultural factors. This is hardly surprising, certainly when considering those whose work I have discussed in the previous pages, because they have tended to be sociologists. In particular, they focus on individuals as 'change agents', or on the role of 'modernizing elites', the progressive members of which are said to provide the impetus to modernize. Generally, the elite are considered to be the agents of modernization and the lower classes as the bearers of tradition, which is normally defined as backward. To some extent, Barrington Moore and Bendix are exceptions in that both emphasize the importance of the political process without necessarily placing the elite on a pedestal. Generally, though, if lower-class norms matter at all, it is because they have to be changed into modern attitudes or because their legitimation of the existing political structure is a necessary condition for social stability. These reasons may help to explain not only the emphasis on individual entrepreneurship but also the wider concepts of innovation and diffusion that have figured, to some extent, in the work of every modernization theorist. They are clearly related, and despite past rancour between evolutionists and diffusionists, they are quite compatible with evolutionism. New ways of thinking and behaving may arise within a society or outside it. Strictly speaking, only the originators are truly innovative; they diffuse the new forms to others for whom they become innovations, to be welcomed or opposed. In this sense, diffusion knows no national boundaries, and diffusion and innovation are different facets of the same process. Both are aspects of social interaction and of culture.

By the end of the 1960s, then, modernization theory was a somewhat hotch-potch collection of rather different perspectives, in which neo-evolutionism, structural functionalism and diffusionism were all to be found. There is no doubt that Parsonian neo-evolutionism was, at that time, in a dominant position, but in the work of Bendix and Barrington Moore there were strong critiques of Parsons, with a much firmer emphasis on socio-economic and political structures and on the links between internal structures and the international environment in which they had to operate. The work of Berger and his associates, coming early in the 1970s, in which insights gained from phenomenological sociology were applied to the process of Third World modernization, serves merely to emphasize the fact that any talk of a unified 'sociology of development' at that time would be to engage in a gross simplification. Indeed, by the end of the 1960s, even as the internal critique of modernization theory was gaining force, a new orthodoxy was already being put forward.

# 3
# Underdevelopment Theory

## Introduction

Just as there is no single modernization theory, there is no one Marxist approach to development. Instead, there is a variety of approaches, originating in classical Marxism and leading to a broad-based 'school' of neo-Marxists, whose collective work has come to be known, at various times, as dependency theory, world systems theory and underdevelopment theory. Nevertheless, although these terms are often used synonymously, it is preferable to use 'dependency theory' to refer to the body of thought concerning 'development' which emanated from Latin America in the 1950s and 1960s, and which was later to lead to a more general view of development, and its opposite, underdevelopment, as key features of the world capitalist system. Dependency theory and world systems theory, despite considerable overlap, can then be seen as constituting underdevelopment theory, which is a reference to all neo-Marxist perspectives which, unlike classical Marxism, regard 'underdevelopment', and not 'development', as the direct result of the spread of international capitalism.

This chapter is primarily concerned with underdevelopment theory but, as with modernization theory, it is necessary to say something about its historical antecedents. Underdevelopment theory (UDT) arose as much as a reaction to classical Marxism as from deeply held objections to modernization theory. Indeed, the growth of UDT has led to a bitter debate within Marxism, and it is no longer possible to make the rather simplistic claim that one is a Marxist and assume that people will know what is meant by the term. Certainly, one may be a Marxist, but of what kind?

At the outset it is necessary to confront a particularly vexing problem. Some theorists insist that Marxism is able to encompass all the social sciences, including sociology, and thus that it is superior to all of them. Marxism then becomes a super social science, containing within its ambit all the theoretical and conceptual refinements necessary for the analysis of the social world. Such a view certainly encourages single-mindedness, both in theory and in political action, and at its best it can lead to a useful focus on the ways in which social, economic and political institutions are connected. In addition, as a political doctrine, many have found it appealing. However, as an overall world view applied dogmatically to all social phenomena, Marxism, in any of its manifestations, does not contain all the answers, and it seems best to regard it as but one of the major theoretical orientations in sociology.

The degree to which Marxism may be regarded as a unitary perspective, superior to all opposition, is related to another, even more pressing, problem: the extent to which aspects of Marxist writing can be extracted and discussed in a wider context. More specifically, when dealing with UDT we need to distinguish contributions to economics from contributions to sociology. To argue that Marxism is all of a piece and cannot be so sub-divided is ultimately to claim for it the status of a privileged account, and to hold a view that is unacceptable even to many Marxists. It is indeed the case that UDT is primarily concerned with economic structures, but it was developed, in part, as a direct challenge to modernization theory and the sociology of development, and my purpose in this chapter is to explore the alternative explanation the theory offers for the development, or lack of development, of the Third World.

## *The Classical Marxists*

It is now commonly recognized that neither Marx nor Engels had much to say about the Third World. Their main interest was the development of Western capitalism and they drew on other societies chiefly for illustrative purposes. As a consequence, Marx did not attempt to analyse the characteristics of non-industrialized regions in any depth; his interest in feudalism, for example, arose because in Western Europe it preceded capitalism. In addition, it is a moot point whether or not he was a committed evolutionist, considering that all societies should pass through identical stages en route to capitalism. Undoubtedly, he was represented as a unilinearist by Stalinist orthodoxy, a view many non-Marxists have been happy to accept and then to criticize, but there is some evidence to suggest that he was a little more circumspect in his approach to historical change, and he insisted that there was no master-key to understanding historical processes (cf. Palma, 1978, p. 888; Melotti, 1977, pp. 1-27; Hobsbawm, 1964, pp. 46-51). That said, however, he appeared convinced of the pervasiveness of capitalism, and it is worth repeating his famous remark that 'the country that is more developed industrially only shows to the less developed, the image of its own future' (Marx, 1954, p. 19).

Certainly, Marx left us no comprehensive theory of imperialism, and it was left to his successors to develop his somewhat contradictory insights. For Marx, foreign trade, along with several other factors, acted to counter the tendency of the rate of profit to fall. Through trade, and its accompanying economies of scale, capitalists were able to increase the rate of surplus value and thus, at least initially, their profits. First through plunder and then through superior production techniques they were able to gain the competitive edge, 'so that the more advanced country sells its goods above their value even though cheaper than the competing countries' (Marx, 1959, p. 238). It is likely that Marx envisaged that the spread of capitalism would result not in imperialism but 'in a proliferation of autonomous capitalism, such as he expected in India and did witness in North America' (Kiernan, 1974, p. 198). As I shall indicate in the following pages, this is really the key issue that divides classical Marxists from underdevelopment theorists: for the former, Third World societies remain 'undeveloped' until they are 'developed' by capitalism, whereas for the latter it is precisely because such societies have been incorporated into world capitalism that their development has been blocked, even reversed, and they have become 'underdeveloped'.

In the opening years of the twentieth century, Marxists and non-Marxists alike addressed the problem of imperialism. In a book which can be especially recommended, Kiernan (1974, pp. 1-68) suggests that Hobson and Angell, both non-Marxists, were of crucial importance. For Hobson (1902), imperialist expansion was a kind of distorted capitalism, in which the chief culprits were arms dealers and war contractors, and capital was exported because of a lack of domestic investment opportunities. The situation could be remedied by increasing the wages of workers, thus providing a much needed boost to the home market. This 'underconsumptionist' thesis was later rejected by Lenin, who nevertheless followed Hobson in emphasizing the export of capital. Angell, too, (1910) criticized the militarism of the Great Powers, yet remained convinced that imperialism brought overall benefit to the colonies, a view which was not opposed to that of Marx.

Of the classical Marxists, it was Rosa Luxemburg who gave most weight to the Third World. In *The Accumulation of Capital* (1951, first published 1913), she asked how it was possible for capitalist accumulation to continue, despite the fact that productive capacity was increasing faster than the capacity of the market to purchase consumer goods. In effect, her answer was the Third World. It was the existence of non-capitalist regions, purchasing consumer goods, supplying raw materials and providing new markets for capital, that kept Western capitalism on the move. In the process, such regions would eventually be absorbed into the world capitalist system, thus increasing the competition for world markets. As Frölich remarks,

> previously the capitalist robbers hunted side by side, but now they begin to squabble among themselves for the remaining non-capitalist space which has not yet been confiscated and for its redivision. This is the age of imperialism (1972, p. 158).

Luxemburg considered that capitalism necessarily involved imperialism and militarism, itself an important mechanism for realizing surplus value, but that ultimately capitalism would destroy itself: it would 'necessarily implode'. However, socialism was not inevitable; much would depend on class action and, in particular, the weapon of the mass strike.

In many respects, Luxemburg anticipates underdevelopment theory, but for her the Third World does not occupy the centre of the stage. Instead, it is the arena in which capitalists fight their battles: 'The stimulus comes wholly from the colonizers, the imperialists' (Nettl, 1966, pp. 835-6). And her argument is not without its problems: there seems to be an obvious flaw in the suggestion that the working class in the advanced countries lacks purchasing power, which is yet placed in the hands of underdeveloped peoples. It seems evident that 'the masses from whom super-profits were extracted would be still less able to buy the products of further investment' (Barratt Brown, 1972, p. 64). In addition, the Third World bourgeoisie could hardly have been large enough to provide an adequate market for capital goods or mass-produced consumer items emanating from the West. Even at the time Luxemburg was writing, there was ample evidence that the Western working classes were benefiting from capitalism. (In parenthesis, if this was so, and if such benefits were gained at the expense of workers in the Third World, we are faced with the possibility of an internationally divided proletariat – a problem for anyone adopting an internationalist perspective and who, like Luxemburg, minimizes the role of nationalism in working class consciousness.)

While Luxemburg was applying herself to the revolutionary cause in Germany, Lenin was similarly occupied with Tsarist Russia. His theory of imperialism was soon to be elevated to something resembling an official creed and heretical texts, like those of Luxemburg, subsequently fell into disrepute.

## Lenin and Imperialism

Lenin's theory of imperialism, incomplete, politically motivated and a synthesis of previous writers, is nevertheless an attempt to explain imperialism. In fact, it soon came to represent received wisdom in classical Marxist theory, from which underdevelopment theory was later to diverge, and for this reason it is necessary to outline its main characteristics.

Imperialism is defined by Lenin as 'the monopoly stage of capitalism' (1965, p. 105). For him it was a comparatively recent development, crystallizing in the 1860s and becoming fully established in the opening years of the twentieth century. In this process, a crucial component was the merger of bank and industrial capital to form finance capital which, for Lenin as well as for Hilferding, was 'capital controlled by banks and employed by industrialists' (Lenin, 1965, p. 52). Through their command over finance capital, the major banks were able to control the use of the means of production and the sources of raw materials, encouraging centralization and 'transforming thousands and thousands of scattered economic enterprises into a single national capitalist, and then into a world capitalist economy (Lenin, 1965, p. 35),

Secondly, Lenin followed Hobson and, to some extent, Luxemburg, in emphasizing the export of capital. Whereas in the 'old capitalism' the export of commodities had predominated, 'typical of the latest [rather than the 'highest'] stage of capitalism, when monopolies rule, is the export of *capital*'. (Lenin, 1965, p. 72; author's emphasis). In the export of capital, the tendency towards monopoly is again evident, both within the advanced countries and in bettering their position relative to the rest of the world. In such countries, 'the accumulation of capital has reached gigantic proportions. An enormous "superabundance of capital" has arisen in the advanced countries' (Lenin, 1965, p. 73).

Thirdly, like Luxemburg and unlike Hobson, Lenin dismissed the idea that this 'superabundance' of capital could be used to increase the standard of living of Western workers, or to develop the agricultural sector:

if capitalism did these things it would not be capitalism; for both uneven development and a semi-starvation level of existence of the masses are fundamental and inevitable conditions and premises of this mode of production (1965, p. 128).

However, at this point Lenin was not entirely consistent, conceding that high profits in advanced capitalist nations enable the creation of 'privileged sections', detached from 'the broad masses of the proletariat' (1965, p. 128). In the same passage, he approvingly quotes letters from Engels to the effect that 'the workers merrily share the feast of England's monopoly of the colonies and the world markets' (1965, p. 129).

Fourthly, imperialism is seen as the logical extension of capitalism rather than as but one of several choices open to the capitalist powers. It is a necessary development of capitalism, and the political and military conflicts of such powers reflect economic interests. Indeed, the imperialists may seek to annexe a region 'not so much directly for themselves as to weaken the adversary and undermine *his* hegemony' (Lenin, 1965, p 109; author's emphasis). That said, however, Lenin is inclined to use 'imperialism' more loosely, for example, when it means 'the partition of the world' (1965, p. 125), and at such times political and economic criteria become blurred.

Finally, and perhaps most importantly, like other Marxists of the period, Lenin had no doubt that imperialism would take capitalism into the Third World, even at the expense of the advanced capitalist powers:

> The export of capital affects and greatly accelerates the development of capitalism in those countries to which it is exported. While, therefore, the export of capital may tend to a certain extent to arrest development in the capital exporting countries, it can only do so by expanding and deepening the further development of capitalism throughout the world (1965, p. 76).

This theory of imperialism is open to criticism on a number of counts. As with Luxemburg, it is still unclear why the 'super-exploited' Third World can provide markets for mass produced goods from the West when the proletariat of the advanced societies (or, at any rate, the great bulk of it) is unable to do so. Indeed, with the benefit of hindsight, is is hardly the case that the latter has suffered worsening standards of living, however uneven its development has been. In addition, it is common to point out Lenin's failure to distinguish one type of colonial possession from another. As Sutcliffe notes, (1972, p. 317), both Hobson and Lenin were somewhat slapdash in their use of evidence linking exports of capital to annexation. When Lenin was discussing British investment in the colonies, for example, (1965, pp. 74-6) he was quite willing to lump Asia, Africa and Australia together, even though it should have been obvious at that time that the nature and extent of British investment varied widely, as did the relationship of colonies to the metropolitan power.

It is relevant to note that Lenin claimed neither that his theory was complete nor that it should be considered separately from other Marxist writing. What he did was to combine 'the dominant tendencies in capitalism observable in a number of countries into a composite picture of monopoly capitalism' (Barratt Brown, 1972, p. 27). In short, we are being offered an ideal type rather than a theory. If this is so, we can consider empirical data, for example, the reasons for colonial annexation, its correlation with the outflows of capital and the profitability of such investment, without having to reject all the assumptions inherent in the ideal type or the value of empirical data when the two do not coincide. This suggests, too, that imperialism may best be regarded as an aspect of capitalism, rather than being synonymous with it. Bearing this in mind, Sutcliffe suggests that imperialism can be approached in three distinct ways:

(1)  By an analysis of the structure of advanced capitalist countries and their expansionist tendencies;
(2)  By examining the relations between developed and under-developed societies, and
(3)  By focusing on the internal structures of Third World societies (cf. Sutcliffe, 1972, p. 320).

Such a scheme is not unproblematic: with the exception of the Socialist bloc – itself a noteworthy admission – it is, in effect, the study of the world and everything therein. However, it does constitute a framework within which we can situate the works of classical Marxism and underdevelopment theory. Like that of Marx, Lenin's contribution to the debate can be placed largely within the first of the above approaches, but some of the major characteristics he isolated have laid the basis for future studies. Such concepts as 'world system', 'dependency', 'unequal development' and 'semi-colonial' are to be found in his work, albeit in an undeveloped form. It was left to the theorists of underdevelopment to build on them, focusing especially on the 'expansionist tendencies' of the advanced capitalist societies and on the relationship between 'developed' and 'underdeveloped' societies. In so doing, they opposed not only modernization theory, but also entered into dispute with more 'orthodox' Marxists.

## Theories of Underdevelopment

Just as 'bourgeois' theories of development were, at least in part, a response to the decolonization process – a political development that led to the application of standard sociological approaches to 'new' nations – so, too, was underdevelopment theory. But it was more than that. Dependency theory, a key element of underdevelopment theory, arose from a growing disillusionment with *economic* strategies for development, especially as they had been applied in Latin America. This rejection was also accompanied by the realization, not confined to Latin America, that classical Marxist analyses were not appropriate in the context of the Third World; they focused on the advanced capitalist nations, whereas UDT was more concerned with relations between developed and underdeveloped societies. By the mid-1960s, when Parsons published his *Societies: Evolutionary and Comparative Perspectives* (1966), and before the second edition of Rostow's *The Stages of Economic Growth* (1971), the attack from Latin America was well under way. It was greatly aided by Frank's popularization of the work of Paul Baran, especially *The Political Economy of Growth* (1973, first published 1957). The date this book was first published is important, for it was three years before *The Stages of Economic Growth*, and all of seven years before the issue of the *American Sociological Review* that heralded the rise of neo-evolutionism (1964). This brief chronology is relevant because it makes nonsense of the claim that underdevelopment theory had to counter an established sociology of development. In fact, it was more a case of the 'cure' being produced before the onset of the alleged disease.

## Baran and Underdevelopment

In *The Political Economy of Growth*, Baran asserted that bourgeois social science gave ideological support to the ruthless exploitation of the Third World that was, in his view, inherent in capitalism. Unlike Lenin, he considered it to be in the interests of capitalism to keep 'the backward world' as an 'indispensable hinterland' (1973, p. 20), which provided the West with valuable raw materials and opportunities to extract an economic surplus. At the start of capitalism in the West, peasants and merchants had been able to accumulate capital rapidly (for Baran, an essential prerequisite of capitalism) but this had not been possible in the colonies. Except for Australia, New Zealand and North America, most colonizers were 'rapidly determined to extract the largest possible gains from the host countries, and to take their loot home' (Baran, 1973, p. 274). According to this view, underdevelopment in Third World countries, as measured by 'the paucity of their per capita output' (p. 267), was a direct result of capitalist development in the West, a relationship that no amount of 'aid' or agrarian reform could disguise. In short, what might be called the see-saw theory of development was born. For Baran, the only way Third World countries could escape from this economic impasse was to withdraw from the world capitalist system completely and introduce socialist economic planning – the 'rational solution' and 'self-evident truth' (1973, p. 119).

In effect, Baran posed a direct challenge to prevailing notions of capitalist development which, for him, had been disastrous for the Third World. Monopolies that had once been considered progressive were now active in keeping wages down, thus inhibiting the demand for their own products, and whilst a general increase in consumption would benefit the entire capitalist system it would spell ruin for any individual company prepared to increase the consumer power of its own workers to the detriment of its own competitiveness. In such circumstances, 'aid' is, at best, a palliative,

> swamped by the rapid growth of the population, by the corruption of the local governments, by squandering of resources by the underdeveloped countries' ruling classes, and by profit withdrawals on the part of foreign investors (Baran, 1973, p. 122).

As the above passage makes clear, Baran did not ignore the internal class structures of underdeveloped societies and he did not suggest that it was impossible to obtain an economic surplus. However, he felt that the actual, rather than the potential, surplus was largely wasted. First, a part of it went to the 'lumpenbourgeoisie', a somewhat indeterminate category which included merchants, money lenders, real estate agents and others he considered to be non-productive and parasitic. Secondly, domestic industrial producers also received some of the actual surplus. However, they were inclined to be monopolistic, thus discouraging competition, and remained content to rest behind high tariff walls. Far from being the traditional, Western type of entrepreneurs, they either sent their profits overseas or engaged in conspicuous consumption of imported luxury goods. The third recipient of the economic surplus was foreign enterprise, similar in many respects to its domestic counterpart but perhaps even more reliant on the export sector. In Baran's view, foreign companies brought few benefits to the 'host' society: investment tended to be from profits made locally (and was frequently in the developed rather than the underdeveloped societies), and most capital goods were imported (thus increasing the metropolitan rather than the local market). In addition, foreign enterprises were inclined to be capital-intensive, providing little employment for local workers, who, in Baran's view, may well have been reluctant to be employed by foreign companies.

> While it may well be true that the natives' reluctance to perform adequately for starvation wages is due to a 'cultural lag' and to insufficient insight into what is good for them, the chances are that their resistance is caused by the simple fact that they are much better off in their traditional ways of life, by comparison with what foreign capital is pushing and pulling them into (Baran, 1973, p. 330).

At the empirical level, the assertion that workers are reluctant to be employed by foreign enterprises may now occasion some doubt. However, the picture Baran paints is clearly at odds with orthodox development economics, stressing as it did (and continues to do) the benefits of foreign investment for the Third World.

Finally, the economic surplus is also taken by the state. The actual mechanisms by which this is done will vary from one state to another, as will the ways in which the revenue is spent. Baran refers to three types of state: first, the directly administered colony, which uses its revenues to develop its resources of raw materials and which operates a 'full belly' policy'; secondly, the comprador, or agent, government, which rules on behalf of Western capitalism, concentrates on developing its military and ideological apparatus, and which caters most for the tastes of the rich and least for the welfare of the masses; finally, the 'New Deal' type of government, which is the arena for competing class interests of national bourgeoisie, feudal and comprador elements, among which the only common factor is nationalism.

All of this is a far cry from orthodox development economics, and the expectation that Third World societies can, with a little diffusion and assistance through aid, develop along similar lines to the capitalist West, always provided that the proper motivation can be aroused or taught. However, it should be remembered that Baran is dealing with ideal types of societies in at least two senses. The first is the more conventional, social scientific sense, where some characteristics of existing societies are abstracted and developed into a 'pure' conceptual tool to be used as an aid in analysis. Here, Baran is quite explicit, and he is fully aware that there are vast differences among capitalist countries, as well as among Third World societies (cf. Baran, 1973, pp. 264-5). However, in a more everyday sense, he refers to an 'ideal' society, a socialist society, without exploitation and with the potential economic surplus fully used for the benefit of the majority rather than for the exploiting minority.

Undoubtedly, there are problems with Baran's thesis. He mentions, but does not develop, the fact that underdeveloped regions may exist within developed areas, and his definition of development may appear a little dated. Against this, however, he clearly has in mind the possibility of a just and non-exploitative society, based on socialism rather than on capitalism. He was perhaps utopian in his view of what could be achieved by Third World societies following a socialist path of development, seeming to suggest that in such societies, or between them, inequality would no longer exist. Allied to this, as Sutcliffe remarks, he places too much reliance on the Soviet model of development, with its emphasis on heavy industry, capital goods and highly mechanized production (cf. Baran, 1973, pp. 96-7). It could also be argued that Baran was against neither Western capitalism nor its diffusion as such:

A peaceful transplantation of Western culture, science and technology to the less developed countries would have served everywhere as a powerful catalyst of economic progress. The violent, destructive, and predatory opening up of the weaker countries by Western capitalism immeasurably distorted their development. A comparison of the role played by British science and British technology in the development of the United States with the role played by British opium in the development of China fully epitomizes this difference (1973, p. 299).

This looks suspiciously like the argument that it is not capitalism per se that has led to the underdevelopment of the Third World but a stunted, imposed capitalism that has failed in its civilizing mission. However, if this was, indeed, Baran's view, it sits uneasily in a book that, generally speaking, seems opposed to capitalism in all its forms.

Baran's book did not win instant approval from established economists. 1957, when it was first published, was not a year in which Marxists were especially favoured in the United States; indeed, it was described as 'a straight Stalinist tract' and 'a predictable piece of Marxist orthodoxy', with the patronizing remark that 'if the book were read by, say, an African student with little knowledge of history, he might seriously be misled' (Sutcliffe, in Baran, 1973, pp. 64-5). And if the effect on economists was minimal, that on sociologists seems to have been non-existent. However, the book was to play an important part in the formation of Marxist and neo-Marxist views of development and Sutcliffe points out that Baran both reiterates and develops the concept of uneven development, and complements Lenin in indicating the importance of the division of the world by the capitalist powers. In addition, the focus on exports, on capitalist competition and on the role of militarism and war are rightly regarded as a continuation of the concerns of classical Marxism. Nevertheless, it is surely an under-statement to claim that, by regarding capitalism as a hindrance to Third World development, Baran's view 'represented a change of emphasis from much previous Marxist writing' (Sutcliffe, in Baran, 1973, p. 100). More accurately, such a view was a downright contradiction to Marxist, as well as capitalist, orthodoxy, both of which tended to argue, albeit for different reasons, that capitalism was, if nothing else, a necessary stage in the development of any society.

## Dependency Theory and ECLA

In the West, Baran was virtually a voice crying in the wilderness. However, there were also rumblings of discontent from the Third World which became increasingly difficult to silence. As Seers remarks, dependency theory is 'very much a product of a particular place and particular historical period' (1981b, p. 13). In Latin America, the Great Depression had shown how perilous it was to rely on export-led growth: when exports were curtailed, growth declined. In any case, by this time it was evident that there was little potential for increasing the value of Latin America's agricultural exports to the industrialized societies. Improved productivity in Western agriculture emphasized the fact that, for Latin America, the terms of trade were becoming unfavourable. In these circumstances, Latin American exports, usually primary crops, were able to purchase fewer and fewer manufactured goods. In short, Latin American was said to be structurally disadvantaged in the world economy. It was this disadvantage, with the corresponding failure of 'national' development, that led Latin American theorists to examine the ways in which their societies were linked to the West. As Palma (1978) makes clear, this involved three inter-connected levels of analysis: the development of an overall theory of underdevelopment, a focus on obstacles to nation development, and a more empirical examination of 'concrete situations' of dependency. At a more practical level, especially after the Second World War, the answer to the problem was considered to be indigenous industrialization, with Latin American manufacturers sheltered behind protectionist barriers, replacing overseas producers. The policy of import substitution, as it came to be known, was adopted in the 1950s by the United Nations Economic Commission for Latin America (ECLA) under Raúl Prebisch. ECLA argued that protectionism, along with state planning, would increase employment and lead to a more efficient utilization of local capital, itself supplemented by foreign investment. The up and coming middle classes of Latin America welcomed this approach, seeing within it the seeds of their own advancement and the decline of archaic social structures (cf. Sunkel, 1977, p. 8; Dos Santos, 1976, p. 71).

Even in the 1950s, when the policy of import substitution was being put forward, it had its Latin American critics, some of whom were within ECLA itself. As Cardoso points out,

> The analysis of dependency situations in Latin America done in the second half of the sixties did not represent new methodological propositions. What happened was that a current already old in Latin American thought managed to make itself heard in the discussions that were taking place in institutions normally closed to it: ECLA, the universities, some government planning agencies, and – last but not least – the North American academic community (Cardoso, 1977, p. 9).

By 1964, ECLA itself was quite clear on the effects of its policy of import substitution:

> Latin America has not achieved a steady rate of economic growth during the post-war period. Only a few years after the end of the Second World War, the rate of development began to slow down. This downward trend became more general after 1955 and by the end of the fifties had led to stagnation in many Latin American countries and in some to a reduction of the absolute levels of per capita income (United Nations, 1964, p. 1).

The fall in price of agricultural exports relative to imported goods, increases in the importation of fuel and intermediate products, along with rapid population growth and inadequate advances in agricultural production, were all held responsible by ECLA for the failure of the import substitution policy. So, too, were such internal factors as the unequal distribution of wealth, income and land.

If ECLA was critical of its own policies (cf. Palma, 1978), other critics were even more forthright. Some blamed ECLA for not having a general theory of Latin American dependency (a view Frank was to develop at length) whilst others focused more on the internal obstacles to industrial growth, especially the failure of Latin American elites to fulfil the role of an industrial bourgeoisie. And still others, emphasizing the diversity of Latin American societies, suggested that specific Latin American countries reacted differently to international capitalism according to their geographical position, natural resources and their particular configuration of class interests. Indeed, proponents of this view conceded that development and dependence were not necessarily contradictory; rather, it was possible to find examples of 'dependent-associated development', that is, a type of capitalism similar to that in the developed countries yet with the latter exercising dominance in the control of profits and in the most advanced sectors of the economy, more often than not through the activities of transnational companies (cf. Cardoso, 1977, p. 207).

Even by ECLA's narrow definition of development – economic growth and increases in per capita income – the policies of import substitution were judged to have failed. For others, too, economic independence remained a dream; social and economic inequalities continued, usually increasingly and, instead of national development, 'the so-called national bourgeoisie who were to have presided over this process have been assimilated by foreign capital' (Dos Santos, 1976, p. 71). Indeed, it was often believed that foreign capital, rather than promoting industrial diversification and export opportunities, led to an even greater dependence on the West, especially the United States. And when import substitution did occur, it tended to be of goods which were hardly vital for national development and certainly did not provide food for hungry people. Expenditure of scarce national resources on such 'unnecessary' products, even if it saved foreign exchange, served also to focus attention on social and economic inequalities. Clearly, ECLA economists were not unaware of these issues: they pointed to the asymmetrical nature of relationships between the developed 'centre' and the underdeveloped 'periphery' and emphasized the importance of internal structures in the development process. Nevertheless, despite increasing concern with income inequalities and land reform, 'as far as policy was concerned, the course of events in the 1960s increasingly passed ECLA by' (Booth, 1975, p. 61).

It was in this context, then, of disillusionment and hurt national pride, that dependency theory arose in Latin America. Although Latin American societies may have obtained their independence before the 1960s, it was felt by many that economically they remained colonies. For a while, the protest was largely contained within Latin America, but it was not long before it was expanded into a wider critique of all capitalist development in the Third World.

## Frank's Critique of 'The Sociology of Development'

Frank, a Chicago-trained economist, writes as a convert to dependency theory, a supporter of the Cuban revolution and as a committed socialist. Much influenced, too, by Baran and ECLA, he set out to confront what was, in his view, the prevailing sociology of development of the late 1960s.

According to Frank, modernization theory was empirically invalid, theoretically inadequate and politically ineffective. He refers, first, to the 'Ideal Typical Approach', in which development is seen to be a change from one type or stage of society to another; as examples he cites Hoselitz, with his use of the Parsonian pattern variables, and Rostow's stages of growth. In Frank's view, neither developed nor underdeveloped societies reveal the characteristics suggested by Hoselitz; particularist modes of orientation, for example, are common in the former, as is universalism in the latter. In any case, he argues, there is no evidence that these characteristics actually determine development and underdevelopment. The Hoselitz thesis is considered theoretically inadequate in that all roles are given equal weight, in that it fails to specify which section of society is the unit of analysis and, most importantly, because it ignores the historical and structural bases of underdevelopment. As a result, Frank was similarly unimpressed by the kinds of policies derived from this approach, and he notes that the Latin American middle class has consistently supported military dictatorships and has grown primarily at the expense of the poor:

> Economic development and cultural change of an underdeveloped country through the promotion and rise of the middle classes (or their pattern variables) has not occurred because, among other reasons, it is physically impossible for it to occur given the structure of the system: it only leads to the further underdevelopment of the majority (Frank, 1969, p. 39).

Whilst Hoselitz does not entirely ignore the structures of underdevelopment, it remains true that for him, and indeed for

Parsons, the empirical development of the Third World was very much a secondary matter. In Frank's view, the same criticism might be made of Rostow's theory of the stages of growth: they simply do not correspond to the past or present reality of underdeveloped countries. In the modern world no country can be described as 'traditional' (Rostow's first stage), and despite capitalist penetration (often over centuries) the 'pre-conditions for take off' have been conspicuous by their absence. Indeed, Frank takes issue with Rostow's analysis of development: 'That England and other countries did not develop by relying on their own efforts has been exhaustively proven' (1969, p. 46).

For Frank, then, the Ideal Typical Approach, exemplified by Hoselitz and Parsons, is utterly unsatisfactory. Such an approach,

'in all its variations, ignores the historical and structural reality of the underdeveloped countries. This reality is the product of the very same historical process and systemic structure as is the development of the now developed countries' (Frank, 1969, p. 47).

Frank's second line of attack is against the acculturation or diffusionist perspective, which seems to suggest that if development fails to occur, it is because within the Third World there are obstacles to diffusion. He denies that development can be introduced into such societies, and suggests that it is not poverty that has prevented underdeveloped societies investing in their own future but the net outflow of capital to the West. In short, the Third World has subsidized the development of the First. The process has been exacerbated by other outflows – of profits and dividends, of skilled labour – and Third World development has been further undermined by its declining share in world trade, through foreign control of its industries and through careful and restricted transfers of technology. In fact, where economic diffusion has occurred it has been to the disadvantage of the underdeveloped countries.

Up to this point, Frank has said little about cultural diffusion, an important concept in modernization theory. Indeed, it is unlikely that he would see much to recommend it, and he notes that those values related to liberal economic theory (most specifically to free trade) have hindered Third World development; similarly, what he refers to as 'social liberalism' has also been detrimental in its influence. Such liberty, for him, 'is the liberty of a few individuals to move, monopolize, and thereby restrict the development of the economic, political and social whole' (1969, p. 60).

Diffusionism, then, especially economic diffusion, is considered by Frank to be empirically invalid in that it does not bring about development in the Third World. Theoretically, it is based on the false notion that underdeveloped societies are made up of two economies, the modern and the traditional, whereas in reality we are dealing with one sub-system of a global economy. Diffusionism is regarded as incorrect because the unit of analysis is incorrect. In such circumstances it will also be politically ineffective.

In his attack on the Ideal Typical approach, Frank directed his attention primarily at Hoselitz and Rostow, both of whom were economists; in his criticism of diffusionism or acculturation he concentrates on economic factors: capital, investment, technology, profits and dividends. The third target of his wrath is psychological explanations of development, such as those provided by Hagen (1962) and McClelland (1961). These may be seen as consistent with diffusionism, in that they suggest that development can occur when individual attitudes are changed, and that such change may be introduced from the outside. As shown in chapter one, similar ideas were put forward by Lerner (1958), with his depiction of a 'mobile personality' and by Inkeles and Smith (1974), in their search for an 'overall modernity syndrome'. Frank's objections to psychological approaches follow the now-familiar pattern: in essence, they ignore the historical circumstances that led to and perpetuated one world economic system in which the Third World functions to develop the First.

Frank aims his critique at the sociology of development. This might appear somewhat odd, given that most of his targets are non-sociologists and that, at the time he launched his broadsides, there was no subject or academic discipline that could properly be referred to as the sociology of development. Nevertheless, it could be argued that the contributions of Parsons that followed Frank's intervention would not have won Frank's approval, and the evolutionism of Parsons, Levy and Lerner, as well as the more sophisticated approach of Berger and his associates, neither dealt with, nor purported to deal with, the underlying economic structures of underdevelopment. In this sense, if for no other reason, Frank's criticisms may be regarded as applicable to the above mentioned. The plain fact is that anyone who is regarded by Frank as a 'bourgeois' social scientist has little to offer. Such theorists, especially those who espouse the traditional-modern dichotomy: 'are intellectual and political schizophrenics' (Frank, 1969, p. 77). These are strong words, typical of Frank's style, and they are not necessarily reserved for 'bourgeois' writers. There have been occasions when Frank has turned, in similar fashion, on those holding ideas similar to his own (cf. Frank, 1975, pp. 65-6 and 1976, pp. 106-7). The question then arises as to what Frank offers us as an alternative.

## Frank and the World System

In many respects, Frank's alternative to the sociology of development is implied in his critique of it. However, he is but one of several writers who can be collectively categorized as theorists of the world system. Dos Santos, Wallerstein, Emmanuel and Amin represent variants on the same theme. In this section, I address the Frankian version, moving in the pages following to a focus on the different emphases within this overall approach. Why start with Frank? Certainly, he was not the originator of a world systems viewpoint; it should be evident that he owed much to dependency theory, to Baran and to ECLA. However, he was the great popularizer: it was his voice – strident, passionate, dogmatic, contemptuous and insistent – to which students of the late 1960s and 1970s responded. How far his work became the 'exemplar' of a new 'paradigm' is a question to which I shall return in the final chapter of this book, but his influence on a new generation of students was immense and, if nothing else, he exemplified the 'radical' protest of the period.

Several maxims may be taken to summarize Frank's position, which appears to have changed but little over the years. First, there can be no theory of underdevelopment that does not take account of the actual history of underdeveloped societies. Any such theory will recognize that underdevelopment is a *result*, a direct result, of relations with capitalist countries and that, far from being 'dual' societies, characterized by a 'traditional' and a 'modern' sector, capitalist penetration has reached far into the 'traditional' hinterlands of Third World societies, thus increasingly enveloping them into the global capitalist system. Development and underdevelopment, then, are aspects of the same system: the world capitalist system.

Secondly, there is a chain of metropolitan/satellite relations in the structure of this world-wide system which transcends national boundaries. Within a country, the hinterland supplies the city and is exploited by it; in turn, the city (often the centre of the export trade) is dependent on the metropolitan countries of the West:

> When we examine this metropolis-satellite structure, we find that each of the satellites, including now underdeveloped Spain and Portugal, serves as an instrument to suck capital or economic surplus out of its own satellites and to channel part of this surplus to the world metropolis of which all are satellites. Moreover, each national and local metropolis serves to impose and maintain the monopolistic structure and exploitative relationship of this system...as long as it serves the interests of the metropoles which take advantage of this global, national and local structure to promote their own development and the enrichment of their ruling classes (Frank, 1969, pp. 6-7).

Thirdly, it is incorrect to argue that industrialization and development occur only when a country is closely linked to the West. The links, which need not be through formal colonization but may be economic, through capital investment and transfers of technology, serve only to reinforce dependence. Countries which once had the strongest links with metropolitan powers are now the most underdeveloped of all. Areas such as the West Indies, North-East Brazil, and the mining areas of Latin America were exploited for their usefulness and then abandoned. With their social, economic and political structures geared to their satellite status, they had no alternative but to 'turn in upon themselves and to degenerate into the ultra-underdevelopment we find there today' (Frank, 1969, p. 13). Citing the cases of Argentina, Brazil, Mexico and Chile, Frank asserts that it was precisely when their links with the metropoles were weak, for example, during the two World Wars, that they were able to initiate 'marked autonomous industrialization and growth' (1969, p. 10). And on the re-establishment of the links development was again stunted. By contrast, Frank points to Japan which, in his view, and despite an absence of natural resources, was able to industrialize because it was not a satellite to any metropole. Interestingly, as I indicated in Chapter 2, it was left to Bendix, a modernization theorist writing at the same time as Frank, to point to the interplay of internal class forces and the international setting during the modernization of Japan.

Fourthly, for Frank the internal class structures of satellite societies are, in the end, reflections of wider economic structures. The Latin American bourgeoisie, or 'lumpenbourgeoisie', as he prefers to call it, includes the traditional elite, merchants, lawyers and industrialists, but Frank generally treats them as an undifferentiated mass. There may be occasional conflicts among them, especially when links with the metropolis are weak, but more often than not their interests coincide with those of foreign capitalists. By the mid-eighteenth century, 'a genuine policy of development did not exist anywhere in Latin America' (Frank, 1972, p. 57); instead, there were 'lumpenstates which never achieved true independence but were, and are, simply effective instruments of the lumpenbourgeoisie's policy of lumpendevelopment' (1972, p. 58). Given this kind of description, it is surprising to find Frank occasionally using social class as an independent factor in his explanations. We learn, for example, that Australian development differed crucially from that of Argentina because of internal class factors:

> Australia did not inherit a class structure like Argentina's. Apparently, as a result of the discovery of gold there in 1858, a working class evolved which proved able to oblige the government to adopt effective policies of protectionism and rural immigration for reasons of self-interest rather than development. It was these policies which made development possible in Australia (Frank, 1972, pp. 55-6).

Later Frank compounds the problem. He suggests that during the World Wars Australia and Canada were both able to exploit the weakening of their links with the metropole and then, because of strong economies, they were able to attract foreign investment in 'technologically advanced development-generating sectors' (1978,

p. 121). Quite why class factors exercised such a crucial influence in Australia but not in Latin America is unclear. One wonders, too, why foreign investment perpetuated underdevelopment in Latin America but had the opposite effect in Australia, Canada and 'Western Europe as well' (Frank, 1978, p. 121). The suggestion that Australia and Canada evidenced 'a special mode of production' (Frank, 1978, p. 121) merely complicates the puzzle, inherited from Baran, still further.

Finally, the history of underdeveloped societies has not been, and could not possibly have been, a duplication of the history of the capitalist West, precisely because of the influence of the Western industrial powers. Indeed, both development and underdevelopment are regarded as part of the world process of accumulation, a process that commenced in the mercantile period (1500-1770), carried through into industrial capitalism (1770-1870) and culminated in imperialism (1870-1930). Throughout this process, the colonies, the semi-colonies and the neo-colonies existed primarily for the benefit of the capitalist metropoles and, as a direct result, became underdeveloped. It is only by breaking these links that genuine development can occur.

In short, for Frank the world is a global economic system, increasingly incorporating the Eastern bloc, made up of a series of metropoles and satellites, in which every metropole feeds off its satellites by expropriating their economic surplus. Development in one area is the direct result of underdevelopment elsewhere, and incorporation in the world system precludes development. This approach, which Frank inherited from Baran, may be referred to as the see-saw theory of development and underdevelopment. It was not new. A similar perspective was employed as far back as the 1940s by Williams (1964) to demonstrate the close links between slavery and the industrial revolution, and was also a characteristic of the dependency theorists of Latin America.

## World Systems Theory: Variations on a Theme

Frank is not the only world systems theorist, but he does serve to introduce themes basic to all world systems theory. Others have developed their own versions, and within the 'school' there are interesting and sometimes important differences. In this section, my aim is to indicate where these occur before going on to a general discussion of the nature of world systems theory.

Perhaps the first point to be made is that all world systems theorists focus on the historical background of developed and underdeveloped societies. This is hardly surprising, given the strong Marxist orientation of the writers in question. It is in the past that we find the basis for explanations of the present. Like Frank, Wallerstein suggests that the modern world economic system developed in distinct historical stages. In his case, there are four (to Frank's three): 1450-1640, 1650-1730, 1760-1917, and the period of consolidation after 1917. It is noteworthy that, for Wallerstein, capitalism as a system existed from the middle of the fifteenth century, thus avoiding the 'problem' of the transition of capitalism and feudalism. This follows from Wallerstein's definition of capitalism, the essential feature of which is 'production for sale in a market...to realize the maximum profit' (Wallerstein, 1979, p. 15). As the world economy develops, so does the division of labour, with specialization increasingly occurring across geographical regions. However, the operation of a completely open world economy is prevented by political and cultural differences and interests. Indeed, regional specialization itself arises from 'attempts of actors in the market place to avoid the normal operation of the market whenever it does not maximise their profits' (Wallerstein, 1979, p. 17).

Amin, too, periodizes changes in the nature of capitalism, which he claims starts as mercantile capitalism, becomes developed, as in mid-nineteenth century England, and then changes to imperialism. In turn, pre-capitalist peripheral countries change, from primitive-communalism to tribute-paying societies and thence to capitalism. Like Parsons, Amin claims that this process is not automatic, and when he notes that fledgling European industries of the Industrial Revolution destroyed the old handicrafts and recruited their labour force he almost outdoes Parsons in his expression of structural-functionalism:

Although this twofold process was accompanied by poverty and unemployment, it nevertheless represented an advance in the development of the productive forces, and the new socioeconomic equilibrium emerging from this process of transition to central capitalism was a higher equilibrium than that of the precapitalist society that existed previously (Amin, 1976, p. 204).

The second key characteristic of world systems theory is that, as components of the system, there are invariably two extreme types of society, perhaps with an intermediate category. In Frank's case, the polar opposites are the metropole and the satellite, with the important rider that a region may simultaneously be a metropole to its own hinterland and a satellite to a more 'developed' metropole. In this, Frank echoes ECLA's description of 'centres' and 'peripheries'. However, Frank's world system not only includes developed and underdeveloped areas, but also those which are 'partially-developed':

> Partial-development has occurred in South Africa, Rhodesia and Palestine, which are occupied by white European immigrants and the indigenous population. The remaining colonies (and semi-, neo and ex-colonies) comprising the vast majority of mankind became underdeveloped (Frank, 1978, p. 11).

The exact meaning of 'partial development' is not clear, and the category itself remains undeveloped, but it appears to refer to a situation in which structural economic change has been introduced by a white settler minority, which has proceeded to monopolize the benefits its changes brought about.

Unlike Frank, Amin focuses on a world economic system divided into two sectors: 'self-centred systems' and 'peripheral systems'. In the former, production is for mass consumption, and there is a social contract between capital and labour which serves to minimize conflict. The system is self-centred in that it possesses its own, internal dynamic, unaffected by external relationships. By contrast, the periphery exists to meet the centre's requirements, which it does mainly through exports, and any capital accumulated is transferred to the centre. Low wage rates and a distorted domestic market, meeting only the demands of the privileged classes for luxury goods, results in the impoverishment and marginalization of the masses. According to this view, participation in the world system exacts a heavy price, involving as it does the decline of small agricultural producers and cottage industries, the semi-proletarianization of rural areas, and unemployment and underemployment. Poverty in the periphery thus functions to maintain and increase wealth among the periphery's privileged classes, and at the core.

Whereas Amin operates with a view of a two-tiered world system, Wallerstein criticizes him for failing to include an intermediate category. For him, although peripheral countries were normally unable to move from their lowly position to core status, they could cease to be only exporters of low-wage products and might begin to produce for part of their domestic market. As a consequence, Wallerstein's world economy has three components: first, core regions with strong states that can enforce unequal exchange relations favourable to themselves; they appropriate surplus value from the periphery, the second system component, which is made up of exploited regions characterized by mono-agriculture and a dependence on the export of low-wage products. Thirdly, we have the semi-periphery, an intermediate category which acts as a buffer, separating the core and the periphery, which produces high-wage and low-wage products. It is exploited by the core but in turn exploits the periphery. The semi-periphery is the arena in which capitalists, especially the transnational companies, confront one another openly and meet socialist alternatives head-on. Perhaps because of this, semi-peripheral states may be stronger than those of peripheral societies and they can, at certain times (for example, during a worldwide contraction of markets) improve the position of the semi-periphery vis-à-vis the core countries. Indeed, Wallerstein specifically relates the strength of state machineries to the structural position of a society within the world economy. At base, it is a reflection of the overall international structure and not 'genetic-cultural' factors. We have, then, a world economic system comprised of core, periphery and semi-periphery, which is kept going by military force, and 'by the pervasiveness of an ideological commitment to the system as a whole' (Wallerstein, 1979, p. 22), especially among those outside the core who nevertheless benefit from the system and its three-layered structure. 'When and if this ceases to be the case, the world system disintegrates' 1979, p. 23). In short, the entire system is sustained by the semi-periphery, which disguises the tensions between peripheral societies and their cores.

Whereas Frank's category of 'partially-developed' societies seems to be restricted to a few areas of the world dominated by white settlers, Wallerstein's number of semi-peripheral societies is considerable:

> The 'semi-periphery' includes the economically stronger countries of Latin America: Brazil, Mexico, Argentina, Venezuela, possibly Chile and Cuba. It includes the whole outer rim of Europe: the southern tier of Portugal, Spain, Italy and Greece; most of Eastern Europe; parts of the northern tier such as Norway and Finland. It includes a series of Arab states: Algeria, Egypt, Saudi Arabia; and also Israel. It includes in Africa at least Nigeria and Zaire, and in Asia, Turkey, Iran, India, Indonesia, China, Korea and Vietnam. And it includes the old white Commonwealth: Canada, Australia, South Africa, possibly New Zealand (Wallerstein, 1979, p. 100).

There are obvious differences between Frank and Wallerstein about which country should be put in what category. Frank, for example, regards Australia, Canada and New Zealand as developed, whereas Wallerstein sees them as semi-peripheral. More importantly, Wallerstein includes most socialist societies in his intermediate category, suggesting that they differ from their capitalist counterparts only in their political role within the world system and in the recipients of their expropriated surplus value. Economically, their roles are identical. Wallerstein's semi-periphery is crucial in the operation of his world system, stabilizing the tensions between the exploiting core and the exploited periphery. The semi-periphery trades with both, fulfilling the dual function of periphery to the core and core to the periphery. In this intermediate position, and with considerable state control over 'economic' decisions, it can 'play' the international market more than core or peripheral societies. It is because it is in this intermediate position within the international economy that its internal structure includes an enhanced role for the state.

Indeed, the third characteristic of world systems theory, which arises from its focus on the international structures of inequality, is its tendency to treat internal socio-economic structures as of secondary importance, even as derivative. Despite some inconsistencies, this seems to be Frank's position. At first sight, Dos Santos (1976) appears to give more autonomy to the class structures of Third World societies, arguing that Latin American dependence is the result not only of the expropriation of surplus by the metropoles, but also of the relatively static nature of their internal structures, which had been 'conditioned by international relations of dependence' (1976, p. 76). Elsewhere (1970), he maintains that the nature of Latin American dependency changed over time; historically, it was caused by colonial domination or financial-industrial control, whereas in the period after the Second World War it was increasingly based on the power of transnational corporations. In both cases, however, inequalities inherent in the international system are exported to the Third World and come to be reflected in their internal structures, which evidence the continuing dominance of traditional oligarchies, vast inequalities of wealth and income and intense exploitation. The rich of the Third World join hands – and interests – with their metropolitan counterparts in the joint exploitation of the Third World's poor. In fact, Dos Santos has arrived at Frank's position, where class interests and class structures are 'determined by the dependence of the Latin American satellite on the colonialist, imperialist metropolis' (Frank, 1972, p. 1).

For Amin, internal structures are similarly constrained by the international context. Despite the fact that Third World social formations evidence different articulations of modes of production, the spread of Western capitalism leads peripheral societies increasingly to resemble one another. Because they exist primarily to satisfy the requirements of the centre, their economic systems indicate extreme unevenness in productivity and in prices and prevent the development of a national capitalist class; instead, the dominant class is that of agrarian capital, in association with 'ancillary (comprador) commercial capital' (Amin, 1976, p. 202). In these circumstances, the drive towards industrialization is led by the national bureaucracy, possibly through some kind of state capitalism, and whatever surplus remains in the periphery is expropriated by this class for its own interest.

Wallerstein's approach to Third World social structures differs from that of Dos Santos, Frank and Amin. He argues that within the world economy there exists a variety of bases for collective action, of which social class is but one example; the others he subsumes under the umbrella term 'ethno-nations', which includes nations, nationalities, peoples and ethnic groups (cf. Wallerstein, 1979, pp. 23-4). Within the context of the nation-state, the traditional unit of analysis, membership of ethnic, racial and other status groups may blur the importance of class membership; however, Wallerstein regards it as crucial to view such examples of collective identification and action within the context of the world economy. Ultimately, class interests cross political boundaries, but within them is a constant jockeying for influence by specific groups (classes or ethno-nations), all of which seek to distort the operation of the world market by carving out special spheres of influence within it:

> Political struggles of ethno-nations or segments of classes within national boundaries of course are the daily bread and butter of local politics. But their significance or consequence can only be fruitfully analyzed if one spells out the implications of their organizational activity or political demands for the functioning of the world economy (Wallerstein, 1979, p. 25).

Internally, the core, periphery and semi-periphery may reveal marked differences, and Wallerstein emphasizes the contrasts of the core with the semi-periphery. He argues that, compared with core societies, capitalist semi-peripheral countries are likely to have a smaller, but better paid, professional sector, along with a relatively small and weak indigenous bourgeoisie, which is often linked to transnational companies based in the core. In addition, they will have a smaller and more poorly paid proletariat with a far larger, but still poor, semi-proletariat, whose income is only partly obtained from wage labour. When dealing with the socialist semi-periphery, he distinguishes it from its capitalist counterpart by pointing to an even smaller, perhaps non-existent, indigenous bourgeoisie. That said, like Frank he accepts that the 'external' bourgeoisie, based in the core countries and probably operating through the transnationals, may exert considerable influence even in the socialist semi-periphery. Indeed, in his view, genuine socialism is unable to develop in a capitalist world economy.

Certainly, this view of Third World internal structures is more detailed and considered than that of Frank or Amin. However, despite the route followed by Wallerstein, he arrives at the same destination: class conflict is essentially an international phenomenon which nonetheless may be blurred by alternative forms of association. This is especially so, perhaps, at the periphery, where

> the primary contradiction is between the interests organized and located in the core countries and their local allies on the one hand and the majority of the population on the other. In point of fact, then, an anti-imperialist nationalist struggle is in fact a mode of expression of class-interest (Wallerstein, 1979, p. 200).

So far, I have attempted to show that world systems theorists differ in their approaches to the historical foundations of the world economy and that they tend to polarize the societies that make up this system, often with the addition of an intermediate category. In their different ways, too, they tend to treat social and economic structures of the Third World as, at root, derivative from the operation of the world market. There is also considerable consensus among them on the mechanism through which international inequalities are maintained. As the fourth characteristic of world systems theory, then, it is necessary to focus on unequal exchange, a topic which, for Marxist economists, involves highly complex issues. It is clear that Amin, Frank and Wallerstein were strongly influenced by the debate on equal exchange, especially by the work of Emmanuel (1972). At one level, unequal exchange merely denotes the inequalities in trading relations between advanced industrial societies and the rest of the world – inequalities that are obvious to everyone. However, it is quite another thing to explain why this unequal exchange occurs. For Emmanuel, the 'bourgeois' theory of comparative costs, that sets out to explain, and usually to justify, the international division of labour, is clearly inadequate. Instead, he emphasizes unequal exchange as the most elementary transfer mechanism, which allows developed countries to begin and to maintain uneven development and asymmetrical trading links in which they are the senior partners. At the heart of his theory is the assumption that whilst capital is mobile across international boundaries, labour is not, and the result is the obvious differences between wages in the Third World and wages in the industrialized West. It follows that because Third World products are produced by people whose labour is relatively undervalued in money terms, the products themselves are relatively cheaper than those produced by the advanced capitalist countries. In turn, this means that the terms of trade are heavily biased in favour of the West, which does its best to 'encourage' the Third World to produce for export. Clearly, one form of encouragement is foreign investment in the Third World export sector. According to Amin,

> This is therefore the framework for the *essential* theory of *unequal exchange*. The products exported by the periphery are important to the extent that... the return to labour will be less than what it is at the centre. And it can be less to the extent that society will, by every means, economic and non-economic – be made subject to this new function i.e. producing cheap labour in the export sector (Amin, 1974, p. 13; author's emphasis).

This version of unequal exchange is not uncontentious. Mandel, for example, criticizes Emmanuel's assumption, shared by Frank and Wallerstein, that capital is internationally mobile; were this the case low-wage countries would be swamped by foreign capital and underdevelopment would not occur. He points to clear, empirical evidence that foreign capital has, in fact, been consistently prepared to accept widely different rates of profit across the world economy, and argues that international differences

> in the value and the price of the commodity of labour power, which Arghiri Emmanuel rightly underscores, are *not causes but results* of the uneven development of the capitalist *mode of production*, or of labour productivity in the world (Mandel, 1978, p. 353; author's emphasis).

If wage rates are the result of uneven development, rather than its cause, they can hardly be used to explain unequal exchange, of which they are but an indication. Mandel's answer to this problem is to point to social structures of underdeveloped countries not, like Frank, as examples of some kind of subordinate capitalism but as 'the specific combination of pre-capitalist, semi-capitalist and capitalist relations of production' (1978, p. 365). It is not that they lack capital, but that this capital is either foreign (with profits subsequently exported) or unproductively invested. And this situation, and thus underdevelopment, will continue for as long as internal Third World markets remain small, indigenous agricultural sectors remain backward, and national capital remains restricted. That this is unlikely to change in the present world economy is a view Mandel shares with the world systems theorists, but the mechanisms of underdevelopment are not, for him, explained by unequal exchange, which is itself a result of underdevelopment and not the cause.

The debate over the concept of unequal exchange is both complex and detailed, and much of it relates to the applicability, or otherwise, of Marx's theory of value to the modern world system. Nevertheless, Frank, Wallerstein and Amin regard it as a key component in the transfer of surplus from periphery and semi-periphery to the core countries (cf. Frank, 1978, pp. 103-10; Wallerstein, 1979, pp. 18 and 86; Mandel, 1978, pp. 343-76; Brewer, 1980, pp. 208-32). The debate among them is not so much over whether or not unequal exchange exists, but what causes it: the sphere of production, the market, or a combination of the two. It is a debate which has much occupied underdevelopment theorists and some of their Marxist critics, as the following pages will indicate.

It is stating the obvious, perhaps, to note that the fifth characteristic of world systems theory is that it treats the entire 'world' as its basic unit for analysis. To be sure, the world in question is generally regarded as capitalist, and there is some disagreement as to how far the Eastern bloc countries are an essential part of the world system. Frank sees them, along with China, as an 'integral part' (1980, p. 182), sacrificing their commitment to socialist revolution in the process. Wallerstein sees them, and China, as semi-peripheral within the world economy, whereas Amin is known to have regarded Mao's China as a model of self-centred, socialist development. He is hardly likely to view post-Mao China in the same light. In fact, Amin's description of the world system is more explicitly structural-functionalist than Frank or Wallerstein. His stress is on the relationship of central and peripheral economic structures within a worldwide process of capital accumulation, and the debate is generally conducted in terms of the operations of systems, the 'needs' of capital and the 'requirements' of capitalism. Indeed, 'each class-divided mode of production determines a pair of classes that are both opposed and united in this mode' (Amin, 1976, p. 23). Furthermore, 'Each of these classes is defined by the function it fulfils in production' (1976, p. 23). Amin's system is the world, made up of core and peripheral societies, every one of which has different articulations of modes of production. Within these modes, there are polarized classes, simultaneously united and divided but all defined by their functions in production. In reality, he recognizes that social formations are more complex than this two-class model implies and yet, even when attempting to deal with empirical complexities, it is hard to escape the impression that, for Amin, the abstract system is the reality. Even when he accepts that economic functions are but one aspect of social organization, Amin's functionalism is unabated:

> A society cannot be reduced to its infrastructure. The way the latter (in other words, its material life) is organized requires that certain political and ideological functions be carried out relevant to the dominant mode of production and the linking-together of the various modes that make up the given formation. These functions may be carried out directly by the classes that have been defined above, or else by social groups that are dependent upon them. The actual structure of the particular society will be strongly marked by these groups (Amin, 1976, p. 24).

Despite the possibility of such functional equivalents, the needs of the system predominate and the constituent parts of the system, be they classes or their functional equivalents, of necessity function to ensure the perpetuation of the system. However, even when dealing with specific geographical areas, Amin is reluctant to 'flesh out' his categories with actual social groups. It is not clear, for example, why village communities in the Arab world were able to resist agrarian capitalism for a long period (cf. Amin, 1976, p. 298), or, more generally, why the growth of a comprador trade sector was restricted by 'phenomena characteristic of the structures of the urban community and of the ideology and culture of the new dominant classes' (1976, p. 299). Culture, values and social structures are clearly intended to be significant, but how or why is unspecified. Similarly, in Egypt, the 'third estate' of craftsmen, clerks and village notables were 'heirs of the traditional culture' (1976, p. 303) and actively opposed colonization at the end of the nineteenth century, yet the nature and content of this 'traditional culture' is ignored. Was it merely a reflection of their opposition to European imports? What was the relationship of this culture to the sphere of production?

In fact, in Amin's world system, the acting agents are categories, defined in terms of their functions in the ongoing process of capital accumulation, whose importance and, more importantly, ideological worth, are clearly signalled in such terms as 'petty-bourgeois social elements', 'petty-bourgeois socialism', 'moderate' nationalism, 'revolutionary peasant nationalism', and so on. What is lacking from the 'whole' and its functioning parts is any conception of purposeful human action occurring within a meaningful, cultural environment.

Wallerstein's system, involving the centre, the periphery and the semi-periphery, is similarly abstract, and Wallerstein is clear that his tripartite division of the world may have little to do with reality:

> I am not arguing that three tiers *really* exist, any more than I am arguing that two poles *really* exist. I am indifferent to such Platonic essences. Rather, I am asserting that the class struggle centers politically around the *attempt* of the dominant classes to create and sustain a third tier, against the *attempt* of the oppressed classes to polarize both the reality and the perception of reality (Wallerstein, 1979, p. 224; author's emphasis).

To return to an earlier point, and at the risk of being accused of being preoccupied with 'Platonic essences', I wonder why we need accept the inclusion of so many different societies in the semi-peripheral category when the category itself is called into question. As with Parsons, an earlier systems theorist, the abstractions of the world system seem, at times, to have tenuous links with empirical reality.

Finally, it should be noted that Frank, Wallerstein and Amin agree on the remedies to be applied to the problems brought about by the capitalist world system. For Frank, the answer is worldwide socialist revolution, spearheaded by socialist countries that have refused to compromise their commitment to socialism by partici pating in the world system. Revolution in one country is not possible. Wallerstein expresses doubts about the validity of existing 'socialist' societies. Where socialist revolutions have occurred, for example, in the USSR, China and Cuba, he concedes that there has been an internal reallocation of consumption, and that the means of production have been nationalized, but asserts that neither these measures nor an increase in self-reliance can alone bring about socialism. State ownership, self-reliance and 'socialism in one country' are not enough:

> Production for use and not for profit, and rational decisions on the cost benefits (in the widest sense of the term) of alternative uses is a different mode of production, one that can only be established within the single division of labour that is the world economy and one that will require a single government (Wallerstein, 1979, p. 91).

In short, genuine socialism requires an entirely new world system. Amin provides the same solution, asserting that 'real, autonomous self-centred development' (1974, p. 16) cannot occur when the periphery breaks the chains that link it to the centre. It is a necessary prerequisite but ultimately it is not sufficient: the aim must be the creation of a 'global socialist society' (1974, p. 9) and the stimulus for this will come not from the centre but from the periphery. Indeed, it is one of Amin's central theses that

> when a system is outgrown and superseded, this process takes place not, in the first place, starting from its center, but from its periphery. Two examples are given to illustrate this thesis – the birth of capitalism in the periphery of the great precapitalist systems, and the present crisis of capitalism (Amin, 1976, p. 10).

It should be noted that when it comes to ascertaining the political possibilities of global socialism, Frank, Wallerstein and Amin are equally pessimistic. Despite continuing crises, the capitalist world system persists, increasingly incorporating 'socialist' societies which compromise their avowed principles and dilute their revolutionary commitment by helping perpetuate a system based on the exploitation of the world's poor by the international bourgeoisie. The single world socialist system remains in the future.

## *Summary*

In Frank, Wallerstein and Amin we have the bare bones of what has come to be known as world systems theory. Clearly, they differ in numerous details, and to some extent focus on different areas, but despite this they have much in common, including a more or less blanket opposition to modernization theory. At the risk of over-simplification, their views can be summarized by stating some key points.

(1)  Development and underdevelopment are essentially as-pects of the same economic process, and the former has been able to occur only by increasing the latter. In fact, this may be seen as an international application of the 'image of limited good' (Foster, 1965), where the world is seen as a cake and where, if one group has a large slice of the good things of life, others have to settle for a correspondingly smaller share. Alternatively, it might be described as the see-saw theory of development.

(2)  Development, regarded as autonomous, self-sustaining in-dustrial growth, is no longer an option for the Third World. The very existence of the world capitalist system means that the development potential of underdeveloped countries is blocked.

(3)  The capitalist world system commenced when Western nations developed trading links with non-European coun-tries, gradually incorporating the rest of the world, in stages, into an international system of exchange. All soci-eties, including those without a history of direct colonial-ism and those claiming to be socialist, are now part of this system.

(4)  The mechanisms by which the world capitalist system is maintained are a matter of some debate, but at the heart of the matter is unequal exchange. In effect, this refers to asymmetrical power relationships whereby one group of nations, the 'developed', is able to gain and

maintain an advantage over the others in the terms of trade which, in turn, reflect disparities in military and economic power.

(5) The world is divided into two or three main groups of nations. On the one hand, there are those who have economic power: the 'developed', the 'centre', the 'core' or the 'metropoles'; on the other hand, there are those who lack influence: the 'underdeveloped', the 'periphery' or the 'satellites'. These regions, or polar opposites in the world system, not only differ in their standards of living but also in their economic and social structures. In addition, for some theorists there is an intermediate category – the 'partially-developed' or the 'semi-periphery' – which refers to those regions that are exploited by the centre but which, in turn, exploit their own peripheries. Put somewhat differently, these are the regions that benefit from the crumbs that fall from the capitalist master's table.

(6) The world is essentially an *economic* system in which the primary units of analysis are institutions that represent different factions of labour and capital. In this analysis, the manner by which surplus value is extracted from labour is crucial, but it is accepted that capitalism in the periphery need not rely solely on wage labour. Likewise, social classes are defined according to their position in the overall system, and social, cultural and political phenomena are, at least in the last instance, derivative from the economic sphere and can ultimately be explained by reference to economic structures.

(7) The transnational companies, in particular, are commonly regarded as the main agents of neo-colonialism, in that they are a vital mechanism in the transfer of surplus from the periphery, or semi-periphery, to the centre. They are regarded by world systems theorists as the epitome of capitalism, having disastrous effects on the development potential of the Third World. They are the prime carriers of capitalism.

(8) The room for manoeuvre of underdeveloped societies is limited. As they have developed only when the links between themselves and the capitalist centres have been broken, or considerably weakened, it follows that their

only hope is to sever such links, as far as is possible, and 'go it alone'. How this is to be achieved varies from writer to writer, but is is generally accepted that a combination of self-reliance and socialism is a substantial part of the answer, perhaps with an increase in co-operation with other socialist countries. Ultimately, though, 'socialism in one country' is not possible, and the only satisfactory long-term answer is an entirely new, non-exploitative socialist world system.

# 4

# Critiques of
# the World Systems
# Perspective

## Introduction

In many respects, world systems theorists went considerably
further than some of their intellectual forbears. Clearly, they
diverged sharply from classical Marxism, which regarded capitalism as a necessary stage in development. In addition, they
extended, and perhaps distorted, the work of the Latin American
'dependentistas', who focused more specifically on the historical development of particular Latin American societies and on
the dialectical relationships between the external structures of
dependency and the internal structures of specific social formations (cf. Cardoso, 1977, p. 14).

It was through Frank, especially, and other world systems
theorists, that dependency came to be seen as a general theory,
thus losing its dynamic components and its emphasis on internal
struggle. Importantly, many dependency theorists were prepared
to accept that some kind of industrialization was taking place in
Latin America, and they examined the ways in which indigenous
social structures were changed in the process. However, the more
open-ended approach that characterized dependency theory has
often been submerged within the world systems perspective,
with Frank generally considered its (unelected) spokesman.
Increasingly, 'dependency', 'world system' and 'underdevelopment' have come to be used synonymously to describe one,
general, approach. Certainly, they differ in scope but nevertheless
their message is much the same.

Critics of world systems theory can, broadly speaking, be divided into two camps: those who argue from a 'Marxist' position and those who do not. A further division may also be made, with considerable overlap, according to the degree to which critics focus on empirical or theoretical issues. In the two sections that follow, the first deals with a number of Marxist criticisms, from both theoretical and empirical standpoints, whilst the second concentrates on non-Marxist objections to world systems theory.

## Marxist Criticisms

At both theoretical and empirical levels, much of the disagreement between 'Marxist' and world systems theorists involves competing claims as to who is putting forward the purest version of Marxism. Indeed, there are substantial divisions between them. Some critics argue that world systems theory is conceptually confused in its use of specifically Marxist categories. It was noted earlier that, from the standpoint of the world system perspective, incorporation into the capitalist world system commenced with Western expansion into the New World in the fifteenth and sixteenth centuries. The clear implication of this position is that the capitalist world system existed well before the Industrial Revolution had taken place in Western Europe. However, it can be argued that incorporation into the Western economic system was not synonymous with the adoption of a capitalist mode of production, a view taken by Laclau with particular reference to Latin America. He suggests that defining capitalism as profit-motivated production for the market – the stance taken by Wallerstein and Frank – is simply inadequate. In so doing, relations of production are ignored and capitalism has become confused with the existence of an economic system. Rather, it should be seen as a mode of production characterized, in essence, by the sale by free labourers of their labour power, which necessarily presupposes their separation from the means of production. Noting that Wallerstein distinguishes between free, skilled labour at the core and coerced, less skilled labour in the periphery, which nevertheless co-exist in Wallerstein's capitalist world system, Laclau is led to exclaim that, in so doing, Wallerstein 'does not appear to be aware of the meaning of "free labour"', and as a consequence has forgotten 'what any Marxist knows' (Laclau, 1979, p. 46). Similarly, Frank, too, could assert that Latin America ceased to be feudal and became capitalist when conquered by Spain only by assuming that a feudal mode of production was incompatible with market penetration and extra-economic coercion of labour. By contrast, Laclau insists that the mode of production is an abstraction and should not be confused with specific, concrete economic systems, which will reveal various articulations of modes of production. He goes on to suggest that commercial capital may operate, and has indeed operated for a very long time, relatively independently within non-capitalist modes of production.

At the heart of Laclau's critique is the claim that world systems theory is based on a mistaken view of the nature of capitalism and, more generally, of modes of production. A similar, but more comprehensive position is adopted by Brenner (1977), who agrees that a market-based definition of capitalism is incorrect. Were this the case, capitalism would be defined by the subjective intentions of individual actors, whose profit motives would be sufficient to bring about a capitalist system. Rather, capitalism should be considered a system of production based on the exploitation of free wage labour in which accumulation, development and innovation are intrinsic to the system and are derived from the prior existence of the free labour force. According to this view, the market itself cannot lead to development or dependence. Instead, the driving force of development, of change from one mode of production to another, is the balance of class forces, itself the result of continuous class struggle. This disagreement with world systems theory is not simply a haggle over definitions, for by arguing that it misrepresents the nature of capitalism and its origins, Brenner is also opposing the idea that development and underdevelopment are causally linked, and that the mechanism linking them is that of unequal exchange. By contrast, capitalist development is

a function of the tendency toward capital accumulation via innovation, built into a historically developed structure of class relations of free wage labour. From this vantage point, neither economic development nor underdevelopment are *directly* dependent upon, caused by, one another. Each is the product of a specific evolution of class relations, *in part* determined historically *'outside'* capitalism, in relationship with non-capitalist modes. (Brenner, 1977, p. 61; author's emphasis).

It is not that Brenner ignores the differences between Third World societies and the industrialized West, or that he denies the existence of unequal exchange. However, they are secondary in the development and maintenance of capitalism which rests on the productivity of its free labour force. In contrast to pre-capitalist societies, capitalism is characterized by competition among producers, whose main method of remaining ahead of one another is to reduce the amount of socially necessary labour time involved in the production of any good. Put somewhat differently, this is achieved 'largely by increasing what we have termed relative, not merely absolute, surplus labour' (Brenner, 1977, p. 68). The process necessarily involves continuous innovation by the competing capitalists, an interesting return to a central concern of modernization theory.

In his insistence that we focus on the sphere of production, and on class relations and class struggle, Brenner reiterates themes which preoccupied classical Marxism and which, in his view, were minimized or distorted by world systems theory. The importance of class struggle is noted, too, by Leys (1977, 1978, 1980), Petras (1978), and Phillips (1977), all of whom accuse world systems theory of treating the process of class formation and class struggle as residual. It is a common complaint: 'Class relations appear in Frank's formulation but they do so as residual analytical categories, lacking in real substance' (Goodman and Redclift, 1981, p. 43). The authors of this text also suggest that, if anything, Wallerstein is even more guilty of removing class struggle to the margins of his analysis. Interestingly, Leys was once an enthusiastic advocate of underdevelopment theory. Applying it to Kenya, he considered it 'an immense advance, politically and intellectually, over conventional development theory' (1975, p. xiii). Only two years later, he was to brand it theoretically repetitive, stagnant, unable to solve or even to formulate problems of development strategy, lacking any practical impact on popular struggle and, perhaps worst of all, susceptible to co-optation by bourgeois developmentalists (1977, p. 92). Furthermore, it had no precise definition of development and exploitation, and used primitive, over-general concepts which were mere inversions of bourgeois theory. Finally, it lacked coherence, and was 'ideological rather than scientific' in that it operated with a concept of social class 'which is ultimately residual and passive' (1977, p. 99; author's emphasis).

Both Leys and Petras argue that world systems theory detracts from a focus on specific national and international contexts of class struggle, and Petras in particular notes that although external linkages are undoubtedly important, they must not be regarded as abstractions; rather, they are elements of 'international class alignments' (Petras, 1978, p. 37). In essence, this is a plea to return to the nation-state as the unit of analysis; indeed, in what might be considered the most damning criticism of all, Petras notes

a tendency among world systems theorists to dissolve the issue into a series of abstract developmental imperatives deduced from a static global stratification system which increasingly resembles the functional requisites and equilibrium models of Parsonian sociology (1978, p. 37).

The relative neglect by world systems theorists of Third World class structures has been accompanied by a disparagement of Third World bourgeoisies, on the grounds that, more often than not, they simply serve the interests of international capital. This results in a curious situation, for national capital and national development, both blocked by international structures of dependency, have come to be regarded as synonymous. As a consequence:

National capital has been given the opportunity to put itself forward as representing the 'national interest' and has been ultimately rejected, not because it is *capital*, but because it is unable to be sufficiently *national* (Phillips, 1977, p. 19; author's emphasis).

In other words, it is not capitalist development as such that has been rejected, but capitalist development orchestrated by non-nationals. As a consequence, if national policies were to be handed over to a properly constituted, native capitalist class, development would then occur. Indeed, it is the lack of such an indigenous bourgeoisie that appears to prompt consideration of alternative possibilities. For her part, Phillips argues that Marxists should stop asking whether or not capitalism can or does promote development and instead concentrate on the nature of class conflict in the Third World. She thus returns us, once more, to a focus on indigenous social structures.

It should be evident that some Marxists are less than content with the theoretical formulations of the world capitalist system. Such quarrels are not about intellectual niceties, even though they involve competing claims about who is closer to the letter or the spirit of Karl Marx. The stances taken in these debates are reflected not only in the choice and presentation of empirical material but also in the political and economic strategies for development in the real world.

At a more empirical level, there are Marxists who maintain that world systems theory is deficient in its interpretation of the available empirical data on Third World development. In short, it is said that development is occurring. Capitalism is fulfilling its historical mission. This position is closely associated with Warren, (1973 and 1980) who contends that in many underdeveloped countries successful capitalist development is a real possibility, and that the chief obstacles to it are not inherent in the relationship of the Third World with the West but rather lie in the 'internal contradictions of the Third World itself' (Warren, 1980, p. 10). Indeed, as indigenous capitalism develops in the Third World it leads to the breakdown of dependency. Opposing the world system view that capitalism brings about the underdevelopment of the Third World, Warren claims that

the empirical data belie this picture and that substantial, accelerating, and even historically unprecedented improvements in the growth of productive capacity and the material welfare of the mass of the population have occurred in the Third World in the postwar period. Moreover, the developing capitalist societies of Asia, Africa and Latin America have proved themselves increasingly capable of generating powerful internal sources of economic expansion and of achieving an ever more independent economic and political status (1980, p. 189).

This stark rebuttal of underdevelopment theory has not been popular among neo-Marxists, especially as much of Warren's evidence is taken from non-Marxist sources. In such debates, it is often the source of the data that is judged, rather than the data's content. Nevertheless, Warren provides ample support for his position, which can be summarized as follows:

(1)   In general, since the Second World War, growth rates in many parts of the Third World have been higher than in the developed countries, with little to suggest that growth has been accompanied by a widening of the gap between the Third World's rich and poor, even though Warren also allows that capitalist development may, in its early stages, result in increased social inequality.

(2)   In several important areas of the Third World, an indigenous capitalist class is actively promoting innovation, accumulating capital and involving itself in manufacturing. In short, it is carrying out the proper functions of a capitalist class.

(3)   Urbanization, especially in Latin America, is a vigorous, albeit unplanned, expansion of the market, which simultaneously increases the division of labour in society and helps to break down the economic isolation characteristic of pre-capitalist societies. Indeed, it generally represents a real improvement in living conditions for rural-urban migrants, and Warren used United Nations' figures to suggest that such improvements, as well as increases in population, are directly related to increases in Gross National Product (GNP).

(4)   Further evidence that the poorer classes of the Third World derive benefits from capitalist development is seen in improvements throughout underdeveloped societies in such diverse areas as education, nutrition, health, mortality rates and housing. Further, Third World elites alone do not constitute the domestic market for consumer durables; instead, available evidence suggests that, with urbanization, the lower-income groups increasingly provide a mass market for such goods as bicycles, radios, television sets, motor cycles and refrigerators. Of course, as Warren is aware, it might be argued that the poor's choice is at fault and that

they have been corrupted by Western consumerism, but he refreshingly and correctly notes that 'it is only those who already possess such goods in abundance who feel it appropriate to suggest that it is undesirable for others to have them' (1980, p. 249).

(5) Although there has been a relative neglect of agriculture in the Third World, this is likely to be a temporary phenomenon. Capitalist social relations and capitalist methods of agriculture have spread rapidly to rural areas, with a corresponding growth in wage labour, increased differentiation among farmers and an expansion in the proportion of agricultural output reaching the market.

(6) Manufacturing is playing a more important role in the Gross Domestic Product (GDP) of underdeveloped societies, and in some parts of the Third World it is as significant as, if not more significant than, in the industrialized West. As a consequence of industrialization, some Third World countries 'now have features far from typical of underdeveloped economies' (Warren, 1980, p. 246).

Warren is not suggesting that all is sweetness and light in the Third World, or that capitalist development is without its problems. Indeed, he recognizes that much of what he says does not apply to the poorest countries of the Third World – countries that have benefited little from capitalism primarily because they have been starved of capital. In addition, his empirical data have not gone unchallenged (cf. Hoogvelt, 1976, pp. 77-85). However, at root, the argument between Warren and world systems theory rests on different approaches to the real and the ideal. Following Baran, world systems theorists have in mind a model, as yet unrealized, of socialist development, whereas Warren and his supporters are looking at the real (capitalist) world as it is, albeit with statistical measures which, they freely admit, are far from perfect. Warren's empirical evidence can be criticized on two distinct grounds: first, he equates growth with development and, secondly, the rapidly growing Less Developed Countries (LDCs) are exceptions. However, as a prominent Warrenite argues,

Neither of these arguments are sustainable. The first is sometimes based on a moralistic expectation that capitalism ought to be nice [or]... on the view that capitalist growth at the periphery is 'distorted', which implies some 'correct' standard type of capitalist growth... The second argument is an illustration of the circularity of dependency theory – all LDCs are dependent, except when they're not (Smith, 1983, p. 74).

More recently, the Warrenite analysis has been applied to Africa, hitherto regarded as classically illustrative of dependency. On the basis of the available economic data, the authors conclude that 'the emergence of capitalist social relations of production constitutes the central dynamic process in a wide range of African societies' (Sender and Smith, 1986, p. 128). There has been a vast increase in commodity production and wage labour, and in domestic and international markets, especially where state intervention has succeeded in providing credit and expanding the opportunities for domestic accumulation. Furthermore, the failure of some African societies to develop is attributed not to a hostile international economic environment but to the deliberate neglect of the export sector, a neglect encouraged by the adoption of policies that stem directly from underdevelopment theory:

The acknowledged precondition for such strategies is a socialist revolution, although the class basis or the political forces which would sustain and support such a revolution are generally ill defined. At the same time, the prospects for socialist revolution in African are systematically overestimated a priori, because of the assumed weakness of the economic and political basis of capitalism. In the majority of African economies, where a socialist revolution is not on the short- or medium-term agenda, these analyses have no practical political relevance, nor can they constitute a basis for the strengthening of progressive political forces (Sender and Smith, 1986, pp. 130-1).

By blaming external forces for internal failures, such 'scape-goatism' detracts attention from class conflict and underrates the importance of the growing African working class. It also undermines the continuing need to focus on working conditions and trades union rights, and 'precludes the construction of economic strategies and specific proposals for state interventions which are rooted in "effective reality'" (Sender and Smith, 1986, p. 132).

The Warrenites argue that capitalist development has always been uneven and stress the dangers in treating the Third World as one bloc. It may be that their critics have a point when they challenge the statistical evidence used to arrive at development indicators, but such quantitative data (birth and death rates, figures of GNP, production, trade, and so on) are available, however flawed. The averages may sometimes be considered unsatisfactory but, when all is said and done, world systems theorists can have few grounds for complaint when they use such all-embracing categories as 'core' and 'periphery', with the possible addition of an equally vague intermediate category floating somewhere between the two. Ultimately, it might be more advisable to examine the external linkages and internal class structures of specific societies, rather than focus on the system as a whole, in order to examine the effects of capitalist development. In fact, this is what Warren advocates.

Marxist critics of world systems theory argue that it is conceptually confused in its definitions and treatment of such vital concepts as capitalism, feudalism, modes of production and exploitation. In particular, capitalism is confused as participation in the world market, whilst the focus on 'exploitation' (which owes little to the Marxist theory of value) is said to have deflected attention from the internal structures of the Third World, thus serving the interests of Third World elites who can then claim to be championing the cause of the masses against Western imperialist interests. It is argued that this is nothing less than 'Third Worldism', which disguises the international aspects of class struggle. The alternative approaches recommended vary according to the theoretical orientation of the critics: some advocate an emphasis on the differential articulation of modes of production, perhaps at a higher level of abstraction, and others, sometimes of a more empirical bent, propose a closer examination of specific class structures and struggles and a more open-ended analysis of socio-economic changes occurring in the Third World. Some of these positions can be reconciled: Emmanuel combines his theory of unequal exchange with the belief that the Third World remains underdeveloped because it is not capitalist enough and needs the technology diffused by transnational companies (cf. Emmanuel, 1982). Other contradictions are more stark: if capitalism is defined, a priori, as the main cause of underdevelopment, it cannot simultaneously be regarded as the driving force of development. And the political strategies derived from these approaches are equally at odds with one another. From a world systems perspective, the only hope for underdeveloped countries is to become, as far as possible, self-reliant, and to link up with other socialist countries (even though none may exist at present) with the ultimate aim of bringing about a new and genuinely socialist world system. Alternatively, if capitalism does lead to development, its expansion in the Third World should be encouraged and Third World governments and workers should give capitalism – and transnational companies – a warm welcome.

The debate has come a long way from the concerns of the classical Marxists, who were interested primarily in what may now be called the capitalist 'centre'. For their part, world systems theorists have studied the relations of the 'centre' with the 'periphery' but at the cost, is is alleged, of neglecting the socio-economic structures of the Third World and misunderstanding the nature of capitalism. It may be that they 'largely ignore historical manifestations of imperialism and are in danger of becoming mere empty formulae of a purely ideological nature' (Mommsen, 1981, p. 140).

However, to go on to suggest, as Mommsen does, that world systems theory may still function to prevent us from becoming complacent with capitalism is perhaps to come close to damning with faint praise.

## Non-Marxist Criticisms

At this stage, one might be forgiven for thinking that if world systems theorists attract so much criticism from those who, at the ideological level, should be their friends, they might do better to rely on non-Marxist support. Interestingly, the non-Marxist opposition has been quite muted. Indeed, at the level of higher education, certainly in the United Kingdom, neo-Marxist approaches (that is, underdevelopment theory, or world systems theory) have tended to become the new orthodoxy and modernization theorists have been remarkably silent. The same might be said of much of the Third World, where many intellectuals have welcomed the suggestion that underdevelopment in their societies can be blamed primarily on the West. In north America, it would appear that modernization theory has continued as if it had never come under attack. In fact, from the overall perspective of modernization theory, there is much in underdevelopment theory that can quite legitimately be questioned.

At the theoretical level, it can be argued that world systems theory is, at base, tautological, a view also taken by some Marxist critics. It is a perspective that rules out the possibility of any exceptions. Were it argued that formal colonialism was responsible for Third World underdevelopment it would be comparatively easy to demonstrate that those who had avoided formal colonial domination were no more 'developed' than other parts of the Third World. However, world systems theory explicitly rules out this kind of division, on the grounds that capitalism has penetrated every Third World society, irrespective of the absence or presence of a colonial background. All may be classified as colonies, 'semi-colonies' or 'neo-colonies'. And it is also the case that the Eastern bloc and China have been incorporated into the world system. Everyone is in same boat, for there is no other boat to be in. Put differently, we are faced with the problem of counter-factuality: if there is no way of demonstrating the opposite to that postulated by a theory, we cannot demonstrate its validity. Faced with this theoretical impasse there is little choice but to resort to blind faith, and it is no accident that world systems theory is often presented in such a manner as to suggest that anyone who does not fully support it is, in effect, a class enemy.

Secondly, it is clear that, at a very general level, to announce a relationship of dependency is to do little more than state the obvious. To some degree, every society is dependent. It then follows that the use of the term to describe a wide variety of relationships between countries may disguise more than it reveals. It has been argued that Canada is economically and culturally dependent on the United States (Levitt, 1968), and this in a journal devoted to furthering understanding of the Caribbean. The implication is clear: somehow, Canada's position is similar to that of islands such as Jamaica, Barbados and Grenada. It could also be argued that Saudi Arabia, Portugal, Guatemala, Haiti and the UK are all dependent on the USA, but this is not very helpful. Dependence on the USA is neither new or unusual. Alternatively, we may decide that, if no one is really independent, it is more accurate to refer to interdependence, but the new term is no more explanatory than the old. Clearly, to assert a relationship of dependence or interdependence is one thing; to specify the mechanisms by which this situation came about, and how, if we so desire, it might be changed, is another problem entirely. Indeed, it has been suggested that dependency theorists are wrong to regard dependency as a dichotomous variable:

> With this approach, the model's proponents clearly imply that 'nondependency' is potentially achievable although they assiduously avoid any definition of nondependence, or any serious consideration of what a nondependent economy would look like (Ray, 1973, p. 14).

As Ray goes on to remark, dependency may be said to exist between the USSR and its satellites, whose class structures have much in common with the capitalist periphery, which leads him to conclude that 'the obvious common denominator is not capitalism, but simple disparity of power' (1973, p. 9). Citing Cuba as an example, he somewhat rhetorically asks how far the country is less dependent on trade with the Soviet bloc than it used to be on the West, and how far its undoubted dependence on the Soviet Union is reflected in acquiescence to Soviet policy on a range of economic and political issues. Surprisingly, Ray omits any reference to foreign policy, where Cuban support has been consistent and active, but his basic point is clear enough: even within the Socialist bloc there are buyers and sellers and disparate power relations, and this is reflected in, and a reflection of, specialization:

> This is simply a condensed statement of the principle of comparative advantage. The principle is valid in both capitalist and socialist world trade, although the dependency theorists seem unaware of this universality (Ray, 1973, p. 16).

Once it is accepted that nondependence is an impossibility, and that there are, instead, degrees of dependency, Ray argues that attention can then be directed at practical policies aimed at reducing dependency. However, although it might be useful to construct typologies, or scales, of dependence or interdependence, there have been few efforts to do so, and those that have been produced, mostly in Spanish and unpublished, are said to have resulted in a formalization of history and have served to distract attention from the dynamic elements of social change (cf. Cardoso, 1977, pp. 14-15). And yet, until the term 'dependence' can be used comparatively it will remain little more than a slogan.

Thirdly, while there is ample justification for the emphasis by world systems theory on international economic structures, which have undoubtedly been underplayed by most modernization theorists, there is more to social life than that. Indeed, this kind of perspective tends to reduce all social action and interaction and culture to the expression or representation of some kind of 'objective' economic interest. Marxist critics point to a failure to deal adequately with social class as it operated within Third World internal structures but they, too, underestimate the importance of culture within national boundaries. It is also the case that culture has international ramifications, a point which world systems theorists do little to develop. There are non-economic links of the 'periphery' to the 'centre' that cannot be ignored, and these will vary according to the specific cultural characteristics of Third World countries. As a perceptive critic of underdevelopment theory has observed,

> emulation as a function of status aspirations on the part of intellectuals and politicians and soldiers seeking a place in the international sun; the envy and resentment which often lies behind that emulation; the effect of the diffusion to the late developer of the ideologies – of egalitarianism or conservatism, or zero growth – which are the product of the rich countries more affluent phases; the similar transfer 'out of phase' of institutions – personnel, management systems, patterns of occupational certification, Parliamentary government and so on. The force of these various causal strands is likely to vary from country to country. Exploitation and the self-interest of the comprador class may explain a great deal about a Kenya or a Guatemala; very much less about a Brazil or an India or a Taiwan (Dore, 1977, p. 17).

World systems theory had little to say about such phenomena; indeed, in the context of this chapter, Dore's comments strike a jarring note. They refer to social processes that operate at a very different level from economic structures, and that yet cannot, or should not, be derived from them. It is not merely that world systems theory says little about such social processes – after all, it has its own priorities – but also it gives the impression that they are irrelevant.

It should be evident that world systems theory virtually eliminates any consideration of social action. The same criticism has frequently been levelled at Parsonian systems theory, a fact which in no way invalidates the accusation. Wallerstein, for instance, defines the social system in economic terms:

> We take the defining characteristic of a social system to be the existence within it of a division of labor, such that the various sectors or areas within it are dependent upon economic exchange with others for the smooth and continuous provisioning of the needs of the area. Such economic exchange can clearly exist without a common political structure and even more obviously without sharing the same culture (1979, p. 5).

Having once defined a social system in terms of the division of labour, Wallerstein goes on to argue that the system boundaries can be likened to a grid, 'that would substantially meet the expectations of the overwhelming majority of actors' (1979, p. 14). In short, the world system is a social system, and social systems are defined according to the degree to which they meet actors' economic expectations. Social actors are, first and foremost, economic actors, and from this foundation one can then analyse other kinds of action which, by implication, rest on economic interests. It must be emphasized that this is an assumption, common in Marxist theory, which is totally undemonstrable. However, it is in this way that Wallerstein and other world systems theorists can by-pass sociological approaches that focus on social action and include consideration of the subjective meaning attached to an action by an individual, or by ideal-typical actors. It is not just that they under-rate the importance of social class; they also place little importance on any social grouping which cannot be defined in terms of the functions and dysfunctions that it serves within the wider (economic) system.

It should be noted that in his conception of world systems, Wallerstein recognizes that varieties of culture exist. Indeed, he distinguishes between mini-systems and world systems: the former are characterized by a complete division of labour within the boundaries of one culture, whereas the latter, be they world empires with a single political system or world economies which contain numerous political sub-systems, evidence a plethora of cultures. However, it should also be remembered that his 'ethno-nations' and other groupings within the world system can really be understood only in terms 'of their organizational activity or political demands for the functioning of the world economy' (Wallerstein, 1979, p. 25). Having once explained the functions of these social groups by reference to the needs of the overall system, it is no longer necessary to look at the content of social action and culture. The idea that, ultimately, economic production to satisfy basic needs can occur only within a predefined cultural context is forgotten (cf. Sahlins, 1976); if not forgotten, it is denied. At a less abstract level, Wallerstein can explain the initial emergence of capitalism in the West only by reference to 'a series of accidents – historical, ecological, geographical' (Wallerstein, 1979, p. 18). Culture is conspicuous by its absence. This passage has led one critic to remark

> This leads one to the conviction (if Marx's and Weber's have not already done so) that intra-societal constellations can be pushed to the margins of a theoretical paradigm only to the detriment of that paradigm itself. (Etzioni-Halevy, 1981, p. 76).

It is ironic, perhaps, that the development of dependency theory led to a focus on non-economic aspects of domination, including cultural aspects. As a consequence, cultural dependence came to be seen as mirroring economic and political dependence. However, if we are to follow this line of reasoning, it clearly cannot be assumed that all cultures are equally incapable of resisting the advance of Western 'consumerism'; some must be 'stronger' than others, and the relative strengths and weaknesses will be important to any Third World government in its attempt to assert national autonomy. It is but a short step from this position to assert, with Seers, that cultural dependence may then be 'of a different, higher order of importance than economic dependence' (1981a, p. 7). It is almost a case of the stone previously rejected by the builders being accorded a key role in the structure of genuinely more independent Third World societies. And when Seers, no friend of modernization theory, goes on to stress the importance of 'the motivation, willpower, judgement and intelligence of actual or potential political leaders' (1981a, p. 11), he is, in effect, reviving interest in a central issue of modernization theory.

Theoretically, then, world systems theory might be said to be tautological, in that it rules out any possibility of exceptions and amounts to little more than a statement of the obvious. At the operational level, the concept of 'dependency' is problematic, and cannot deal adequately with the specific relationships widely different countries of the Third World have with capitalist and socialist 'cores'. It thus disguises as much as it can explain. In addition, by eliminating the need for a close examination of crucial intra-societal phenomena, for example, social action and social class formation, and the cultural contexts within which they occur, it can provide only a partial contribution to our understanding of development and underdevelopment. More simply, if we are presented with a perspective that treats as secondary all questions of nation and nationhood and the wide variety of social groupings found throughout the Third World, and which also considers culture as a derivative of international economic structures, we are being offered an approach that is, at best, less than adequate, however convinced and committed its adherents may be.

Finally, it is necessary to comment on non-Marxist objections to the empirical basis of world systems theory. In fact, there is almost total agreement with Marxist critics that development can and does take place in the Third World, and that it is directly linked to the formation of close ties with the 'core' societies. Indeed, it is when these ties are broken or weak that the 'underdevelopment' of the periphery is increased. This, in essence, is the position of Platt, an economic historian whose findings directly conflict with those of Frank, and whose work can be taken as representative of 'bourgeois' opposition to world systems theory.

116

Platt argues that for the period 1860-1920, the decades following independence from Spain, it is simply incorrect to assert that Latin America was incorporated into the world economy as a dependent trading partner.

> Independence from Spain did not, in practice, transform Latin America into a major exporter of foodstuffs and raw materials to the outside world. Nor did it bring Latin America into the market as a large importer of manufactured goods. The reason was simple. Western Europe, within itself, its colonies, southern and Eastern Europe and the United States, was fully supplied both with its foodstuffs and with its industrial raw materials. Latin America could sell nothing to Europe, so that it could buy nothing in return (Platt, 1980a, p. 115).

What Platt is asserting is that it was the lack of trading links with Europe that gave Latin America of this period its characteristics of underdevelopment. It was genuinely peripheral in the world economy, both independent and self-sufficient 'against its will' (1980a, p. 117). Further, in the same way that there was an absence of strong trading links, Latin America also experienced a shortage of European investment. Indeed, before the construction of the railways, the needs of Spanish American industry were met primarily from domestic sources; even when European finance was required for the railways this was forthcoming because of an attractive return on investment, and not because it was hoped that the railways would lead to the development of the export sector. In Argentina, for example, the railways were developed in order to serve the internal market. 'It was fifteen years or more before either line made much impression on Argentina's exports to Britain' (Platt, 1980, p. 121).

He goes on to argue that it is mistaken to attribute great importance to the development of Latin America as a market for European manufactured goods. Up to the 1860s, much of Latin America was in no position to pay for such imports, and after this period the failure of indigenous industry need not be explained by recourse to the structures of dependency. Instead, it was the result of factors internal to Latin American societies: the shortage of skilled labour, a lack of exploitable raw materials and industrial fuels, small domestic markets and a scarcity of capital for large-scale industry. In these circumstances, it was natural for Latin America to develop by creating 'agricultural, pastoral, or mineral wealth' (1980a, p. 123), and by providing processing plants for such products as grain, meat, sugar, cotton and leather.

In effect, Platt denies a central tenet of dependency and world systems theory when he asserts that the failure of Latin American societies to develop their own industrial base was primarily the result of internal factors rather than being conditioned by international economic structures. Unsurprisingly, this view has been challenged on several grounds (cf. Stein and Stein, 1980). It is alleged that Platt under-emphasizes continuity in the structures of dependence, which were established during Spanish colonialism and continued into the first few decades of Latin American independence. Although trading links with the West were much affected by political chaos, both national and international, which followed independence, trade statistics are said to support the view that Latin America remained closely linked to Western Europe. The export of new products, for example, sugar, hides and dyestuffs, further served to bring other Latin American societies, notably Cuba, Argentina and Venezuela, into the international economy.

Much of the debate is over the significance of trade statistics, which both sides agree should be treated with caution. The Steins argue that in the period 1820-1850, Latin American imports of British goods represented 86.5 per cent of those imported from Britain by the United States, and that such imports, especially textiles, had a debilitating effect on Latin American economies which, unlike the USA, were unable to develop their own industries. In addition, they accuse Platt of ignoring the continued importance to Latin America of the mining sector, for example, silver exports from Mexico, in the post-independence period. Platt's response is to suggest that the 1820s was an atypical period, one of 'intense excitement in Latin American trade' (1980b, p. 148), and that if the period 1831-1860 is taken, the figures indicate that, when compared with the USA, Latin America, even including Brazil, was importing a far smaller proportion of British products, at no time more than 56 per cent. Indeed, with the exclusion of Brazil, for which Platt was criticized by the Steins, the figure falls to approximately one third. And Platt adds that any evidence of the continuing importance of silver exports from Mexico does not indicate a sound foundation for a healthy trading relationship, as Mexico had little else to offer. As a consequence, 'the argument that the impact of Britain on the economy of Mexico was critical for its growth is unsustainable' (Platt, 1980b, p. 148).

However, the debate between Platt and the Steins is not only about trade figures. They also accuse him of omitting Brazil, Cuba and Peru from his analysis, despite the fact that they were important trading partners of Britain in the period 1820-1850, and suggest that he misrepresented evidence from other sources in order to bolster his case. In fact, his position is portrayed as thoroughly misguided:

> Thus, excluding major areas of Latin America, relating others to a nebulous 'sometimes' dependency, disregarding or misrepresenting the economic history of yet others (Venezuela, Chile, Colombia), and above all overlooking mining in colonial and postcolonial Spanish America while ignoring the social and political complexities of the Iberian empires in their internal and external relationships, Platt ideates an autonomy that can only appear fanciful to the scholar seeking to understand the history of this part of the world (Stein and Stein, 1980, p. 140).

A non-historian should enter this quarrel with caution. However, given that the disagreement is over how far post-independent Latin American societies were autonomous, it is perhaps worth noting that neither Platt nor the Steins actually define 'autonomy'. Although the Steins criticize Platt for implying that it should be equated with the absence of trade, they do not provide their own definition. Instead, both sides exchange facts and assertions, carefully selected to support their own position and taken from a wide range of available data relating to a vast geographical area and an immense variety of polities and economies. What is autonomy? How far can any society participate in international trade, which invariably involves asymmetrical links, before it should be classified as dependent? What is dependence? These are the underlying questions and they remain unanswered.

Clearly, the economic data concerning the development or underdevelopment of Latin America or, indeed, anywhere else in the world, may be interpreted differently. As the above discussion demonstrates, the debate may often be of a highly technical nature. It may be the case, too, that dependency theory is sometimes too general in its treatment of foreign investment, failing to recognize that different types of foreign investment, for example, in extractive industries, domestic industries, or in the expansion of local markets, may have a different impact on economic development, and that the measures used to assess this development may be less than adequate (cf. Ray, 1973, pp. 11-12). The fact, is, however, that on empirical grounds alone, world systems theory has not gone unchallenged. Indeed, when critics also point to the failure of dependency theory to deal adequately with the transfer of technology (Ray, 1973, p. 13), and with the role of values and diffusion in development, (Safford, 1978, pp. 253-5) we are back on familiar ground: that which was once occupied by modernization theory.

## Developments in Underdevelopment Theory

In recent years, there has been a noticeable tendency for enthusiasm about underdevelopment theory to decline. In part, at least, this is a result of some of the criticisms that have been outlined in this chapter, and it is now fashionable to reassess dependency and world systems theory, and to question whether it has, or should have, survived. In addition, the rapid economic growth of 'newly industrializing countries' (NICs), such as Brazil, South Korea, Taiwan and Singapore, has prompted further re-examination of the possibilities of capitalist development in the Third World. Undoubtedly, underdevelopment theory has much to its credit: it has concentrated scholars' attention on international economic structures and has led some to examine the existence of class interests across national boundaries. It has prompted a renewed interest in the meaning of development and, furthermore, it has given Third World students of development a common cause, arising from their concern with the 'underdevelopment' of their own regions by the West. Nowhere was this radicalization more evident, perhaps, than in the reaction to Rodney's *How Europe Underdeveloped Africa* (1972), a book designed primarily to raise the political consciousness of African students and made more relevant by the author's assassination in Guyana in 1980. These merits of underdevelopment theory must be recognized but so, too, must its limitations. The focus on world systems was partly rooted in Latin American dependency theory, but involved a far greater degree of generalization, at both conceptual and geographical levels, with a corresponding failure to retain a sense of the historical specificity of any one Third World society. One response to this 'systematization' of dependency theory is to return to the more limited objectives of the dependentistas and pay closer attention to specific societies and the various ways their internal class struggles are dynamically inter-linked with the ever shifting but continuously-present inequalities of the international order. Here, the 'internal' tends to be given equal weight, at the very least, with the 'external', and domination and struggle, intrinsic and necessary as they are in society, are not carried on by the impersonal forces of a system but are, instead, experienced, lived and exerted by social groups and classes who are, in the process, the recipients and agents of social change. This, at any rate, is the perspective of Cardoso, who rejects the notion of a formal league table of dependency in favour of 'improvements in the quality of historical-structural analysis' (1977, p. 21). It is a perspective which preserves a sense of the limitations of dependency theory and avoids

the simplistic reductionism so common among the present-day butterfly collectors who abound in the social sciences and who stroll through history classifying types of dependency, modes of production, and laws of development, with the blissful illusion that their findings can remove from history all its ambiguities, conjectures and surprises (Cardoso, 1977, p. 21).

This position is echoed by Palma who, after comprehensively surveying the dependency literature, concludes that no single, overriding theory of dependency is possible, and that there can be no universal strategy for development. Latin American societies are part of the world capitalist system, but differ considerably in their social and economic structures, their natural resources and their geographical importance. As a consequence, the 'external' and the 'internal' are systemically linked:

The system of 'external domination' reappears an an 'internal' phenomenon through the social practices of local groups

121

and classes, who share its interests and values. Other interest groups and forces oppose this domination, and in the concrete development of these contradictions the specific dynamic of the society is generated (Palma, 1978, p. 910).

Significantly, Palma goes on to quote Cardoso in support of this view. However, for Palma, dependency is best regarded as a methodology for studying 'concrete situations of dependency' and, like Cardoso, he warns us against any attempt to make it into a general theory which can be applied to all underdeveloped societies.

Neither Cardoso nor Palma deny the overall usefulness of the concept of a world capitalist system, but they argue that the operation of this system is understood best through smaller scale, less theoretically ambitious, empirical studies. Such a response is, in a very real sense, a reaction, a proposal to return to a more historically specific form of analysis which reiterates the central role of human agency in social change. The desire to retain this focus and yet to situate human action within a social system is not a new one in sociology, and it is an issue which will be discussed in the following chapter.

The 'Warrenites' also advocate a return – in their case to a classical Marxist view of imperialism as the means by which capitalism, albeit unevenly, is introduced into the Third World, gradually but irrevocably leading to the transformation of pre-capitalist modes of production, with the concomitant growth of national bourgeoisies, who take over the historic mission of their metropolitan counterparts. As the preceding pages have indicated, this position, which has much in common with 'bourgeois' modernization theory, is diametrically opposed to the central tenets of underdevelopment theory and has generated intense, not to say acrimonious, debate amongst Marxists of different persuasions. In the remainder of this section, I want to dwell on two themes that arise from the development-underdevelopment debate: first, the increased preoccupation in some circles with the concept of mode of production, a preoccupation which involves a heightened level of theoretical abstraction, and secondly, a renewed interest in social class and the state which is an attempt to deal more concretely with the specific characteristics of Third World social formations.

## Modes of Production and Their Articulation

The concept of mode of production was central in the debate between Laclau and world systems theorists, in which the latter were said to use an inadequate conception of capitalism arising, in turn, from a poor definition of the mode of production. Indeed, earlier analyses of the European transition from feudalism to capitalism also centred on changes in the mode of production (cf. Ruccio and Simon, 1986). More recently, there has been disagreement as to whether or not Indian agriculture has become capitalist. In essence, it has been suggested that the notion of a capitalist mode of production should be refined, as it were, to include two sub-variants, enabling us to refer to a 'colonial mode of production' and a 'post-colonial mode of production', both of which co-exist within a world wide capitalist system dominated by the West. Attempting to combine the insights of Laclau and Frank, Alavi (1975) emphasizes four crucial characteristics in the capitalist mode of production: generalized commodity production, a free' labour force, the extraction of surplus value and class relations. In a fully fledged capitalist mode, commodity production is found throughout the system, there is a supply of free wage labour and the surplus is appropriated by the bourgeoisie. By implication, class conflict is primarily a struggle between the bourgeoisie and the proletariat. Alavi first contrasts this pattern with the feudal mode of production and then notes crucial differences to be found among the various modes, as summarized in Table 1. In the colonial mode of production we have a mode which might best be defined as deformed: extended reproduction has been imposed from the outside, leading to a relative openness in trade with the metropolitan centre but a closed or 'disarticulated' internal economy. Commodity production is also generalized but again imposed from outside, and although a high proportion of the labour force might technically be regarded as 'free', in fact it remains highly dependent on rural landowners. Indeed, Alavi does not rule out the possibility of serfdom in the colonial mode of production, as occurred in Eastern Europe from the sixteenth century onwards, which evidenced what he describes as a 'proto-colonial mode of production' (Alavi, 1975, p. 173). Any surplus is appropriated by the foreign bourgeoisie, and the pattern of class struggle involves all subordinate classes,

**Table 1** *Alavi's Modes of Production*

| | Feudalism | Capitalism | Colonial | Post-Colonial |
|---|---|---|---|---|
| *System characteristics* | 1 Simple reproduction for landlord's conspicuous consumption | 1 Extended reproduction; surplus invested | 1 Deformed, extended reproduction; externally imposed; surplus invested externally | 1 Less deformed extended reproduction; more surplus invested locally |
| | 2 Closed, localized production | 2 Internally and externally open | 2 Internally closed; externally open | 2 Still subordinate but less closed internally; externally open |
| *Commodity production* | Local production and appropriation | Generalized commodity production | Imposed generalized commodity production | Modified generalized commodity production; increased proportion for local market |
| *Labour force* | Unfree serfs | Free wage labour | 'Free' labour still dependent | Continues unfree? |
| *Surplus* | Absorbed by master | Absorbed by bourgeoisie | Absorbed mainly by foreign bourgeoisie | Shared by foreign and local bourgeoisie |
| *Class conflict* | Master vs. serf | Bourgeoisie vs. proletariat | Peasant militancy. All subordinate classes vs. landlords, local and foreign bourgeoisie. Comprador bourgeoisie; weak indigenous bourgeoisie | Increased collaboration and convergence of interest of big local and foreign bourgeoisies |

*Source*: adapted from H. Alavi (1975).

especially, in India, a militant peasantry, in opposition to an alliance of foreign and local bourgeoisies (both comprador and indigenous) with large landowners and rich peasants. In class terms, 'the alignments are the structural alignments and the conflicts of the colonial mode of production; not those of the feudal and capitalist modes' (Alavi, 1975, p. 190).

Alavi maintains that this type of social formation, exhibiting all the characteristics that have come to be associated with under-development, is a sub-variant of capitalism, to be understood only as a part of a wider, international system, from which it originates and by which it is maintained. Undoubtedly, it is a capitalist mode of production, but equally certainly it differs in crucial structural features, detailed above, from what might be described as orthodox metropolitan capitalism.

Finally, Alavi suggests that changes in the Indian economy, dating approximately from the time of political independence, brought about an increased role for the indigenous bourgeoisie which, although still subordinate to overseas capital, was thus able to keep an increased share of the surplus. In addition, there was a simultaneous widening in the domestic market for Indian-produced commodities, developments which together resulted in a greater degree of autonomy for Indian capitalists, and which have been of sufficient structural significance to enable us to refer to a change from a colonial to a post-colonial mode of production.

The distinction between colonial and post-colonial modes of production, which is to include political as well as economic structures, is considered by Alavi to be a useful one, highlighting areas obscured by dependency theory:

We would suggest that the concept of the colonial mode of production and that of the post-colonial mode need to be explored in these other contexts also, to lead us towards an adequate conceptualisation of the structure of the contemporary capitalist world (Alavi, 1975, p. 193).

What Alavi is arguing is that the concept of a capitalist mode of production should be expanded to include Third World variants. These may come to possess some autonomy but nevertheless remain subordinate to the overall capitalist 'centres', which continue to extract the major, albeit reduced, share of surplus value. However, quite how much this kind of argument is able to highlight is questionable. It is at least as likely to obfuscate the issues. There is no obvious reason, for instance, why the colonial and post-colonial modes should be classed as separate modes at all, and Alavi's position involves considerable contradiction as he also recognizes them to be local segments within an overall, capitalist mode. Provided it is accepted that the mode of production is an abstraction, a pure type, it is only to be expected that empirical reality will diverge from it. In any case, it is difficult to escape the conclusion that, for Alavi, the colonial mode of production may be a transitional phase, leading in some (unspecified) circumstances to the post-colonial mode, which is closer to the pure type. The fact that class alignments vary over time and place across the Third World in no way invalidates the model.

Secondly, Alavi confuses the existence of Third World societies, which have defined political boundaries, with the operation of the world capitalist system which, though bounded, need not, and certainly does not, treat political or national boundaries as insuperable barriers to its operation. Indeed, from a world system perspective, a national boundary is no more relevant than any other, and even established capitalist 'centres' contain regions that may be, and at times have been, considered underdeveloped. This is not to suggest that perceived national, cultural or ethnic boundaries are unimportant; however, it is possible that the concept of mode of production is an unsuitable tool with which to analyse them. Ultimately, the obvious importance Alavi attaches to national issues, for example, the role of the indigenous Indian bourgeoisie, owes more to his concern with India as a nation than to the deficiencies or otherwise in the concept of mode of production. Here, he shares the 'Third Worldism' which also characterizes world systems theory.

Thirdly, there is a temptation to equate the capitalist mode of production with the capitalist world system, or 'imperialist mode of production'. It is one which Alavi considers and resists:

> In what sense can we postulate a unity of world imperialism? Would such a unity be premissed on a conception

of its homogeneity or do we assume a hierarchical unity of imperialist countries, say, under the hegemony of the United States. Or, yet again, do we recognise their disunity and the existence of inter-imperialist rivalries. Whatever the fact may be, clearly we cannot settle it a priori, by definition (1975, pp. 190-1).

This is too vague. In itself, the concept of mode of production does not necessitate homogeneity of individual economies, politics, culture, or anything else. Indeed, insofar as capitalism involves unequal development hierarchy is presupposed, and classical Marxists actually anticipated the growth of different capitalist centres, their disunity and their rivalries. In addition, it is not clear which 'fact' cannot be settled by a priori definition: the unit of analysis, be it a capitalist mode of production, a world system or an imperialist one, is of necessity postulated in advance. 'It' exists simply because it is theoretically defined, and the ensuing model is then used to analyse empirical 'reality'. Any rejection of the model must be founded on the belief that it is no longer a useful analytical tool: to argue that it does not exist in reality is merely to state the obvious. What matters is whether or not the conceptual edifice is adequate for the task in hand. Alavi concludes that existing formulations of the capitalist mode of production are of too little value in explaining the social and economic structures of India and, by extension, the Third World, and thus adds his two sub-variants. The question then arises as to whether or not the refined concept of mode of production is more useful than its predecessor, and there is little evidence that it substantially increases our understanding of the relationship of Third World societies to Western capitalism. In a subsequent publication, Alavi refers to

a single peripheral capitalist mode of production in which the various classes are all located, the metropolitan bourgeoisies having a structural presence in these societies (Alavi, 1983, p. 83).

This would appear to be the post-colonial mode of production under a new title. Once again, there is 'no structural contradiction between these competing classes', all of whom share a common interest in the continuation of the capitalist order. The state itself enjoys considerable autonomy, as it functions to mediate among these competing, but non-antagonistic, interests.

> Thus the post-colonial society, while being capitalist, possesses a class configuration and a state that is distinct from those found in advanced capitalist countries as well as in countries under colonial rule (Alavi, 1983, p. 83).

These refinements to the concept of the capitalist mode of production may actually distort the meaning normally attributed to it by Marxists, and this is clearly recognized by Alavi, who admits that his colonial and post-colonial modes are not totalities, possessing 'structural coherence though not completive unity' (1975, p. 191). He then regarded the search for an alternative terminology as 'a semantic exercise', but Marxist critics are unlikely to be so easily persuaded or to find the notion of a 'peripheral capitalist mode of production' any more acceptable.

At a lower level of analysis other problems remain. It is not at all clear how the central characteristic of a post-colonial mode – the increased significance of the indigenous bourgeoisie – comes about, yet this is the issue that separates the Warrenites from world systems theory. It is the crucial factor in the movement from dependent to a more autonomous capitalism, and one which Alavi's reformulation of the problem completely avoids. And to argue that 'capitalist' agriculture in India could develop only within the imperialist system, with a 'structural correspondence of interests' (1975, p. 189), is simply to restate the view that the only possible kind of development in the Third World is dependent development.

Despite Alavi's attempt to fuse the insights of Frank and Laclau, his introduction of new modes, or sub-modes, of capitalist production does little to clarify the debate. It restates the continuation of dependency, albeit in terms different from those used in world systems theory, and fudges the problem of how dependent capitalism in the Third World can be transformed into a more autonomous, indigenous capitalism. It is no longer a question of whether or not agriculture in India, or anywhere else, is capitalist, but what brand of capitalism it represents, and how far it has to go before it is succeeded by another member of the same species. Capitalism remains a system, but the problem is now the number of capitalisms, or sub-systems, within it, and how they are interrelated, not only with one another but also with modes of production that historically or logically precede them.

The relationship of modes of production was a central focus in the structuralism of the French Marxists, especially Althusser (cf. Kahn and Llobera, 1981). In brief, Althusser argued that the later works of Marx were a radical advance on his early writing, and served to introduce a new, theoretically self-contained, philosophy of dialectical materialism in which knowledge was the product of theoretical practice and which contained within itself its own validation. The key component of this practice, read by Althusser into the later works of Marx, was the social formation, within which modes of production interacted, any one of which could be dominant at a specific time. Although the economic sphere would be dominant 'in the last instance', the ideological and political spheres also possessed 'relative autonomy', and the social formation contained structures of all three, hierarchically ordered internally and among one another. All interact or 'articulate' – a term which, though not apparently used by Althusser, expresses both their inter-linkages and their manifestations – and this process can be understood only from within the discourse of Althusser's historical materialism.

Althusser's work was more specifically applied to the Third World by, amongst others, Rey and Taylor. Unfortunately, most of what Rey had to say is currently unavailable in English and, for this reason, I shall quickly summarize his views before proceeding to a closer examination of Taylor's contribution to the debate. As described by Foster-Carter (1978), Rey sees the articulation of modes of production as a process which occurs in three stages. Initially, capitalism links up with, and reinforces, pre-capitalist modes in the sphere of exchange; as neo-colonialism develops, however, production becomes increasingly important and the pre-capitalist modes are increasingly subordinated and subverted by capitalism. At the final stage, apparently not yet reached in the Third World, pre-capitalist modes completely disappear and capitalism reigns supreme. According to this view, while there are a great variety of 'articulations', this is mainly because of differences in and among pre-capitalist modes of production.

As Foster-Carter suggests, this type of analysis, although useful, creates problems: it is unclear how far violence or, indeed, any other kind of conscious human action, affects the transition from one stage of development to another, and it is also unclear how we can ascertain when capitalism has finally 'taken root' in the Third World. Foster-Carter goes on to argue that because Rey distinguishes between (an unmodified) capitalism from 'outside' and (an increasingly modifiable) capitalism 'inside' the Third World, the 'inside/outside' distinction itself becomes problematic. Although Rey stresses the unitary nature of capitalism,

> very many Marxist writers on the Third World take as their point of departure precisely the *lack* of homology between capitalism's effects in its countries of origin on the one hand, those to which it was exported on the other (Foster-Carter, 1978, p. 229; author's emphasis).

It seems to me that this criticism begs the question of what is to be articulated with what, and the nature of the 'whole'. However, in Foster-Carter's view, Rey's approach to the articulation of modes of production necessitates a complementary focus on a world system, with its inter-linked and unequal units. Elsewhere, Bradby considers that Rey is, in effect, arguing that the Third World functions to serve capital's needs for raw materials as well as the needs of individual capitalists for (temporary) competitive advantages in commodity production (cf. Bradby, 1975, p. 152). The system thus remains, and in the course of its transition (or evolution?) through various stages it becomes increasingly complex.

The 'systemic' aspects of variously articulating modes of production is also evident in the work of Taylor, who considers that modernization theory and underdevelopment theory provide equally unhelpful explanations of capitalist penetration in the Third World. Indeed, he sees the latter merely as an inversion of the former, equally determinist and reductionist, and equally prepared to compare a 'real' Third World with some kind of potential, or desired, future order. For him, as for Rey, Third World capitalist social formations are transitional formations, 'structured (or determined in the last instance) by an articulation which is produced largely as an effect of imperialist penetration'

(Taylor, 1979, p. 103). As a result of the interplay, or articulation, of different modes of production, they evidence a 'dislocation' in their economic, political and ideological structures. Indeed, the prior existence of non-capitalist modes makes it inevitable that capitalist development in the Third World will be restricted and uneven, and the nature of such structures is determined by the success of capitalism in penetrating non-capitalist modes and, conversely, by the strength of the latter in resisting this penetration.

At the economic level, the co-existence of different modes of production results in different world experiences which, in turn, are reflected in social classes and in their ideologies, all of which demonstrate the continuing tension between the once-dominant non-capitalist mode and the requirements, often competing, of the capitalist mode. Where imperialism has been restricted to the extractive and processing sector of the economy, its political and ideological influence may be similarly constrained. However, where Third World agricultural products and capital are essential for industrial capital, capitalist penetration in all sectors is increased.

It is important to note that the 'articulation' of different modes necessarily involves an interrelationship; for example, the existence of plantations requiring seasonal labour may benefit capitalists in other sectors of the economy who can then keep their wage costs low. A similar function is performed by villages from which wage workers commute. By meeting at least some of the subsistence needs of the workers, the countryside thus supplements incomes provided in the urban centres.

The articulation of different modes is not restricted to the economic sphere. Taylor often cites the elders who were the dominant class in the lineage mode of production, once found in West Central Africa. Before the onset of capitalism, their power was derived from the receipt of surplus labour, in exchange for which they provided wives and slaves. However, as colonial authorities enforced wage labour, and with it the decline of village production, it became increasingly difficult for young men to provide the dowry in labour form. Instead, it was paid in cash, which had been earned through wage labour as migrant or seasonal workers. In this way the elders, although deprived of some of their power over the process of production, were able to accumulate capital which could then be invested in capitalist enterprise. They thus gained access to a new form of wealth,

> which can only exist as a result of an articulation of the eco-
> nomic instances of two modes of production – an articulation
> that is made possible by the continuing resistance of the lineage
> modes to capitalist penetration (Taylor, 1979, p. 230).

As further examples of the economic linkages of different modes of production, Taylor mentions massive urban unemployment and the development of a 'semi-proletariat', both of which followed the separation of agriculturalists from their means of production, and he also notes the co-existence of different labour forms and divisions of labour which vary according to the extent of capitalist penetration.

Just as the economic structures of Third World capitalist social formations reflect the interaction, or articulation, of different modes of production, so, too, do their social structures. As capitalism extends, the proletariat is increasingly differentiated. A small, well-trained labour force in capital-intensive industry is soon supplemented by a less-trained supply of migrant labour, whilst in the more established, labour-intensive sector of artisan production, controlled by national capital, producers continue to work along traditional lines. At the base of this hierarchy, we have the urban mass, the 'semi-proletariat', whose members experience very different work situations and, as a consequence, vacillate considerably in their political ideologies. This four-fold classification of the proletariat is, for Taylor, quite specific to Third World capitalist social formations.

The peasantry, too, is highly differentiated, with varying involvements in wage labour, subsistence and plantation production, depending on the extent to which the agricultural sphere has been penetrated by capitalism and the degree to which the 'semi-feudal' mode of production has been able to resist its incursions. In a sense, the rural and urban sectors are linked through the activities of the petit bourgeoisie, considered by Taylor to be stronger in the Third World than where capitalism is developed. They are crucial in commodity distribution but, again, are differentiated: some members of this class tend to specialize in the retail of imported goods, whilst others deal primarily with local produce, a division which will be reflected in their support for different strategies of development and different factions of capital.

Divisions among capitalists also vary, according to the degree to which foreign capital has penetrated the social formation, especially the agricultural sector, and depend, too, on the size of the domestic market. However, the class of national capitalists may not be clearly distinguishable from the previously dominant landlord class; here, much will depend on the success of the latter in resisting the spread of capitalism in the countryside or, alternatively, in forming new areas of influence as capitalists themselves. Nevertheless, it is likely that national capital will conflict with the comprador bourgeoisie, which by definition is tied to foreign capital, and as a consequence of their positions within the class structure these classes will have different political ideologies and economic strategies.

Finally, and irrespective of the economic strategies followed, the Third World formation will contain a large class of 'state functionaries', not only to implement development plans but also to provide work for the urban unemployed. In addition, an increasing number of educators is required to inculcate skills necessary in the capitalist divisions of labour, to socialize individuals into the equally necessary legitimating ideology, and to enable the population to cope with a further intensification of capitalism. At the political level, employees of the state depend on those who control the state and, to safeguard their interests, tend to favour alliances of national and comprador capitalists. However, they continue to retain links with the non-capitalist mode, in which they originate and with which they continue to interact, and the ensuing tensions make this class politically volatile and 'less analytically predictable' (Taylor, 1979, p. 252).

It should be emphasized that in Third World formations there is little rigidity in class alliances, which are continually changed in reaction to the progress of capitalist penetration. In the early stages, for instance, foreign capital requires the assistance of the dominant non-capitalist class, which will co-operate provided its own interests are not threatened. However, when international capital requires an expansion of the capitalist mode into the agricultural sector, new alliances with other classes, perhaps including national capital, may be required to further limit the power of the semi-feudal landowners. The process is fraught with difficulties and contradictions and may become out of control, in which case there is a return to the old alliance, often with the assistance of the military.

As we would expect, the articulation of different modes of production leads to a state of flux at the level of ideology, with ideologies from various modes co-existing and changing as a result of developments in the economic and social spheres. New ideologies arise from the introduction of the capitalist division of labour, to legitimate the new social classes and their equally new life-styles, and from attempts on the part of the previously established classes to check the spread of capitalism. Old institutions, too, are transformed: the extended family, for instance, may continue to reproduce an ideology more appropriate to the lineage mode but which is now also required to legitimate migrant labour. Once again, changes in ideological structures and practices will depend on the ability of capitalism to extend into the non-capitalist mode and on the ability of the various modes to defend and reproduce their own economic, social and ideological institutions.

It must be said that this is a comprehensive approach to Third World capitalist social formations, all of which (and everything therein) can be analysed by reference to articulations of modes of production. In addition, it is refreshing to learn that it is simply inadequate to 'read off' ideologies and political practices from the economic sphere, even though Taylor does not always escape this tendency. The complexity of the Third World is reflected in the seemingly infinite variety of ways in which international and national capital can relate to, and be linked with, non-capitalist modes of production. However, it remains the case that, 'in the last instance', the economic determines the political and the ideological, and it is hard to escape the conclusion that the development of capitalism, uneven and restricted though it might be, is still inevitable. Indeed, the fact that Third World capitalist social formations are 'transitional' carries the implication that they are moving to another, more developed, type of capitalism. Taylor does suggest that they contain within their structures the possibility of socialist development, but this is given no detailed consideration. In any case, if they are not moving to the complete dominance of the capitalist mode of production, and they are not becoming socialist, one has to assume that their versions of capitalism, still restricted and still uneven, amount to dependent development by another name.

Like Althusser, Taylor operates with a theoretical perspective, considered by both to be objective and scientific, which might best be described as 'realist': the causes of economic phenomena in the Third World are not revealed through the empirical examination of self-evident 'facts' but can be determined only by reference to a pre-established, and exclusive, theoretical construct:

> *any economic phenomenon* one analyses in a transitional Third World formation is a phenomenal form, the *determinants of which* – the articulation of a mode of production or its elements in another mode – *are not manifest in its appearance*. Consequently, rather than stating that a phenomenon, such as the different forms taken by labour-service, is the result of the existence of two modes of production and the ways in which they are inter-related, we can now go on to state more rigorously that it is *the result of an articulation of different modes of production, and that this articulation is structured by the reproductive requirements of the capitalist mode of production on the one hand and the resistance of the non-capitalist mode of production or its elements on the other, with both the requirements and level of resistance changing over time* (Taylor, 1979, p. 228; author's emphasis).

The theoretical construct in question is Althusser's dialectical materialism, a theoretically comprehensive and self-validating 'problematic' which (allegedly) is not commensurable with any other mode of discourse. By definition, other modes of discourse are ideological. In effect, this amounts to a claim of theoretical omnipotence which cannot be justified; it can only be believed or disbelieved.

In fact, although he rejects modernization theory and under-development theory as inadequate, it is not clear how far Taylor's position represents a completely different 'paradigm'. Certainly, there are times when he is happy to draw on work carried out from other perspectives in support of his own case, as when he enlists Frank to reinforce his view of the relationship of national and metropolitan capital in Latin America and of the beneficial effects of isolation from foreign capital (cf. Taylor, 1979, p. 225).

135

More generally, Taylor presents us with at least two competing systems, or sub-systems, capitalist and non-capitalist, both of which have their own internal divisions and contradictions and compete with one another for economic and political influence. In the 'non-capitalist mode of production' we are provided with a concept not dissimilar to that of 'traditional' structures, be they economic, political or ideological, and in the capitalist mode of production we have another version of 'modernity'. Indeed, the process whereby the dominant mode of production in the social formation articulates with practices of the non-dominant mode, or modes, is much akin to the dynamic equilibrium frequently found in Parsonian theory. Furthermore, Taylor often refers to what modernization theory calls diffusion, albeit by another name:

> Thus, during each phase of extension, the various ideologies in which these dominant classes live their relations with other classes and fractions subordinate in the class structure begin to gain ideological dominance in the major institutions of the Third World formation (Taylor, 1979, p. 270).

Of course, it is understood that the capitalist mode of production does not have everything its own way. It may encounter 'blockages', for example, where 'the existence of clearly demarcated classes is constantly blocked by the continuing reproduction of the semi-feudal mode' (1979, p. 243). At such times, when the two systems come into conflict, all the mechanisms to bring about a new equilibrium are brought into operation:

> When, however, the reproduction of the dominant mode of production becomes blocked by the emergence of a new mode of production (as an effect of imperialist penetration), the articulation of practices has as its object to transform those appropriate to the previous mode of production, to restructure them in relation to the reproductive requirements of the new mode of production (1979, p. 227).

In short, 'traditional' structures may act to block the development of 'modern' institutions, with the resulting formation of new institutions that are neither 'traditional' nor 'modern'. We have returned to the 'prismatic society' (cf. Riggs, 1964).

Taylor has no need to refer to a colonial, or post-colonial, mode of production but, like Alavi, his Third World social formations have similarly distinctive, and similar, economic and social structures. However, it is the comprehensiveness of his concept of social formations which allows him to describe virtually everything and anything in the Third World as the result of the articulation of modes of production or their elements. In his system, or sub-systems, balance and counter-balance, action and reaction, incessantly occur without any specific consciousness or deliberation on the part of human actors. Social action and interaction occur within classes or fractions; relations with other classes are lived within ideologies. Actors are categories, class members, or the supports of other classes or class fractions, and respond to the 'needs' or 'requirements' of articulating modes of production. Despite his use of empirical data, Taylor's system is a theoretical construct and can only be analysed theoretically. Nevertheless, it is a system which has a tendency to evolve, to pass through transitional phases, and with an implicit contrast of a (developed) capitalist mode of production with a non-capitalist (underdeveloped or undeveloped) mode, and a seemingly infinite number of combinations, including 'semi-feudalism', in between. Whilst this kind of approach highlights the undoubted variety found in and among Third World societies, it adds little to our understanding of them, and offers even less to those who wish to derive appropriate policies from its theoretical formulations.

The work of Alavi and Taylor may be seen as a continuation of the debate between Frank and Laclau over the nature of capitalism and the concept of modes of production. Indeed, the 'articulation' question is considered by some to have become central in any Marxist understanding of the nature of modern capitalism (cf. Wolpe, 1980, pp. 1-43). Whereas Alavi was also prompted by an interest in the degree to which Indian agriculture had become capitalist, Taylor attempts to provide a more general theoretical framework with which to analyse the extension of capitalism throughout the Third World. Both were led, in their respective projects, to some consideration of social class and the state. Alavi emphasized surplus expropriation, the form it takes and the class or classes who benefit, whereas Taylor examines the articulation of economic, political and ideological structures within a context of interrelated modes and competing system requirements. Both regard Third World societies as transitional, with distinctive socio-economic structures that result from their colonial histories. Undoubtedly, both approaches take us further than world systems theory, where classes in the Third World are frequently portrayed as stereotypical shadows of their metropolitan counterparts with the state, a mere servant of Western capitalism, dominated by the comprador bourgeoisie and foreign capital. Against this, Alavi and Taylor, in their different ways, point to the possibility of a more independent capitalism with, in some circumstances, a genuine national bourgeoisie, although both also seem to imply that Third World capitalism will nevertheless continue to be dependent.

## An Illustrative Note on Class and State in Africa

When dealing with the linked issues of class and state, there is a perennial problem of applying concepts and categories which arise in the analysis of Western industrial society to the Third World. Consequently, much has been written on the nature of social class, including the peasantry, and on the role of the state in underdeveloped societies. Indeed, the inability of world systems theory to deal with such questions served to intensify these debates, which continue unabated in a wide range of social scientific journals and other publications with a specific focus on the Third World. This can be illustrated by reference to the *Review of African Political Economy* (ROAPE) which was first published in 1974. If offered a Marxist perspective, thus countering what its editors considered to be 'the orthodoxy of bourgeois social science' (vol. 1, p. 3, 1974), and explicitly acknowledged that Africa was integrated into a global capitalist system. However, aware of the over-generalizations that often characterize world systems theory, there was also a recognized need to 'develop theoretical insights into the specificity of the social formations that underdeveloped capitalism gives rise to' (vol. 1, p. 3, 1974). These concerns are reflected in subsequent issues of the journal, the pages of which contain frequent debates on the possible development of an indigenous or national bourgeoisie, the nature of the ruling class and the role of African bureaucracies.

Over the years, some contributors to ROAPE have argued forcibly that a class of national capitalists is emerging in parts of Africa, most notably Kenya, Ghana and Zimbabwe, and that, in the case of Kenya, for example, such developments may have commenced in the pre-colonial period. Indeed, in Kenya after political independence, the state has actively encouraged this process to continue, allying itself with national capital against the interests of foreign capital. Opponents of this view consider it, at best, simplistic, if not completely wrong, and cite empirical evidence to demonstrate that the state, in fact, operates primarily to meet the requirements of foreign capital alone, or of foreign capital in alliance with national capital, but always against the interests of the exploited classes.

Whereas discussion of the growth, or otherwise, of an indigenous African bourgeoisie tends to have focused on Kenya, considered by many non-Marxists to be a capitalist 'success', the issue of the class nature of African bureaucracy has centred on Tanzania. The reasons for both emphases are not difficult to find: politically, it is important for some Marxists to demonstrate that Kenyan 'capitalism' is an unsuitable model for other African states to emulate; for political reasons, too, the failure of 'African socialism', the *ujamaa* experiment in Tanzania, also has to be explained so that in future its mistakes will not be repeated. The explanation is generally achieved by reference to the role of the Tanzanian bureaucracy, which is categorized as a local bourgeoisie in partnership with metropolitan capital in the joint exploitation of the peasantry. Indeed, the entire Tanzanian leadership, including President Nyerere, was branded

> a class of African bureaucrats, intellectuals and traders... a clique consisting of a few bureaucrats that commands all powers, and below it a massive bureaucratic apparatus has been erected to ensure the total control and domination of the entire population (Tabari, 1975, p. 93).

Other contributors suggest that such a view ignores 'progressive' elements among the Tanzanian bourgeoisie, underrates the moderating influence of Nyerere and, by applying Marxist concepts too rigidly to Tanzania, loses sight of the probability that 'any transformation will have to be the brainchild of the bureaucratic elite' (Mahleka, 1976, p. 83). Indeed, there is also resistance to the notion that colonial and, more particularly, post-colonial states somehow require a stronger, more coercive, 'over-developed' state sector than metropolitan capitalist 'centres'. The idea that the 'bureaucratic bourgeoisie' should be seen as

> an entrenched ruling class is an unreliable starting point for further analysis... the contradictions of the situation are obscured by this lumping together of different elements in the state apparatus with the idea of the dominant class and specifically also with the undifferentiated 'petty bourgeoisie' (Leys, 1976, p. 48).

Clearly, how far African societies (and, by extension, other parts of the Third World) possess a 'ruling class' is a matter for debate. It may be, as von Freyhold suggests, that the concept of the post-colonial state needs further refinement. Following Poulantzas, she distinguishes between the (local) 'governing class' and the (metropolitan) 'ruling class', where the former exercises political control in the interests of the latter, and she adds the further category of 'supportive classes', who lack control of the state apparatus but nevertheless benefit from its policies. According to this schema, classes are defined by the functions they carry out, and in the Tanzanian context von Freyhold identifies the (African) *nizers* as partners of the metropolitan bourgeoisie:

> Seen over a longer period the socialism of the *nizers* was in practice a set of strategies which expanded their power vis-à-vis the submerged classes, gave them the means to build up an intermediate class which supports them and put them into a position that made them a viable partner to the metropolitan bourgeoisie (von Freyhold, 1977, p. 88).

These kinds of debate highlight the problems encountered when referring to a 'bourgeoisie' in the African context. Confusion is compounded by the addition of yet more classifications: not only must we contend with ruling and governing classes, but also with metropolitan, national, domestic, bureaucratic, religious, industrial, administrative, rural, urban, regional, organizational, public sector, managerial and political-commercial bourgeoisies, to name but a few! At issue is the extent to which such terms can usefully be applied in the African context, and the extent to which Marxists should regard a national bourgeoisie (if they can find one) as an ally in the battle against metropolitan capitalism. Who is the enemy? In general, most contributors to ROAPE seem to take the view that, ultimately, there is a need

> to conceive of the political struggle as directed against local as well as external class enemies. Moreover, it is instructive to recall that whatever the relative weight of 'international', 'bureaucratic', 'national' or 'petty' bourgeois interests within a ruling block, in our view, the state is essentially a vehicle for the continuing domination or exploitation of the oppressed classes (Cliffe and Lawrence, 1977, p. 5).

This is clearly opposed to the idea that the state is primarily a battleground for competing interests, or a supporter of 'national' capital against 'metropolitan' capital. What is to be done, politically, in response to this state of affairs is unclear, but the answer appears to be a worker-peasant alliance against the 'ruling' and 'governing' classes, preferably led by the 'proletarian party which is the seat of proletarian ideology' (Shivji, 1975, p. 17), with the aim of introducing self-reliant socialism. It is a state of affairs also advocated by world systems theorists; indeed, it is an aim which unites underdevelopment theorists of all persuasions. The problem is not really in the desired destination but in the route to be followed.

It must be emphasized that, in many respects, ROAPE is an excellent journal which has made an admirable contribution to our understanding of African societies. The debates within its pages are, in effect, a continuation of those described in this book: capitalism or no capitalism? Marxist or non-Marxist? Growth or development? And they cover much the same theoretical ground as this and the preceding chapter, with similar disagreements over the nature of the empirical evidence. As in other formulations of world systems and underdevelopment theory, some issues are avoided. Few are prepared to question the alternatives to capitalist industrialization, and the main units of analysis are often theoretical constructs that are applied only with difficulty to the 'real' world. The nature, aspirations and culture of peasants – rich, poor and middle – are usually ignored and so, too, are those of urban dwellers. There are exceptions, for example, an excellent discussion of hidden forms of resistance among African workers (Cohen, 1980), but such gems are rare. All too frequently, theory becomes a substitute for research and serves to separate the analyst still further from the analysed.

Some of these problems are evident in the work of Bernstein, a serious and sophisticated theorist who attempts to examine Third World capitalism ' in terms of the categories and methodology of Marx's analysis of the capitalist mode of production in *Capital*, which remains the starting-point for any scientific investigation of present-day capitalism' (Bernstein, 1976, p. 11). A prominent contributor to the pages of ROAPE, Bernstein was considerably influenced by articulationism and the modes of production debate. Having dismissed his own earlier, and somewhat bland, view of development and underdevelopment as 'radical' and 'ideological' (1976, pp. 9-12 and 13-30), he argues that under-development theory has been unable to produce an adequate theory of capitalism, despite its use of Marxist categories. Instead, like modernization theory, it has a 'unitary conception' of Third World social formations (Bernstein, 1979, p. 89). Neither advanced capitalist economies nor underdeveloped societies should be regarded as autonomous; if they are so regarded, this ignores the international nature of capital movements, markets and pro-duction. Bernstein's primary interest is the peasantry which, he argues, should be located in the context of its relations with the state and capital, relations which are mediated through household production. Using Tanzania as illustrative of the more general issues involved, he concludes that although forms of peasant production remain, they have been transformed by increased commoditization of production within the capitalist system, which provides the overall structure for peasant relations of production. Nevertheless, the peasantry is not fully capitalist: peasants con-tinue to own the means of production, albeit with constraints as to what they produce and in what quantity or quality, which emanate from different forms of capital and the state. In addition, peasant households are based on the needs of simple reproduction and 'a logic of subsistence' (Bernstein, 1977, p. 63), rather than on a need to appropriate surplus value, and when faced with increased prices for goods necessary for consumption peasants will either reduce their expenditure on such items or intensify their own production to meet the increased costs. They could do both.

In general, Bernstein concentrates on the 'middle' peasants, who need neither to sell their own labour power nor to purchase that of others. Some 'rich' peasants may be considered capitalist because (by definition) they can purchase superior means of production and/or labour power. However, they are less likely to be orientated to accumulation and more likely to invest in trade or transport – that is, in circulation rather than production. At the other end of the spectrum, 'poor' peasants (again, by definition) are unable to reproduce through household production alone, and need to sell their labour power. They are a 'rural proletariat in the process of formation' (Bernstein, 1977, p. 67).

According to this view, then, there is 'no single and essential "peasantry"' (1977, p. 73), just as there is no single model of peasant class action. Instead, we have a differentiated peasantry, subject at different times and places to a variety of constraints but always within a capitalist mode of production, characterized by unevenness which structures social relations but continues to 'allow' peasants to own their means of production.

These issues are further developed in Bernstein's analysis of the relations of the Tanzanian peasantry to the state. Both the colonial and (especially) the post-colonial state followed a 'modernization strategy' aimed at increased yields, a more developed infrastructure, increased economies of scale and greater specialization (Bernstein, 1981, p. 48). In an agrarian society, such a strategy is inevitably directed at the peasantry. Nevertheless, 'pre-capitalist social and ideological relations' (that is, family, kinship and tradition) limit further capitalist development, despite the efforts of a post-colonial governing class which, lacking an economic base, is poorly articulated, inefficient and manifestly unable to 'capture' the peasantry. For its part, the peasantry has resisted the incursions of the state, vaguely defined as 'an ensemble of apparatuses and practices' (Bernstein, 1981, p. 56), by falling back on 'individualized household production', a form of production actually reinforced by the policy of villagization.

Bernstein's work is illustrative of an approach in which the role of theory is supreme, and it is difficult to see how his application of Marx's concepts to Tanzania leads to any kind of explanation, even though he asserts that, when correctly applied, they are the defining feature of any 'scientific explanation'. Put differently, this is a claim that only Marxists, and Marxists of Bernstein's persuasion, can be truly scientific, and it is likely to appeal only to those who have already been converted. The categories are so general and the argument so abstract that little is done to clarify the nature of the peasantry, the state, or capital, in Tanzania or elsewhere.

Recently (1987), Bernstein's position has again changed. He has accepted the view (cf. Gibbon and Neocosmos, 1985) that he is guilty of 'peasantism', that is, of conceptualizing peasants as transitional, functional to capital and in possession of a distinct 'logic', and agrees that it is better to regard peasants as but one type of petty commodity producer within the world capitalist system. According to such a perspective, Tanzanian 'peasants' or, rather, 'middle peasants' are analytically in the same category as the capital-intensive wheat farmer of the United States who relies only on family labour. And they are in good company:

> we make no distinction between capitalized or noncapitalized petty commodity producers, between the low or high levels of technological endowment of such enterprises. Thus, our category may include, for example, both household firms of software/hardware computer manufacturers as well as middle peasants (Gibbon and Neocosmos, 1985, p. 171).

'Rich' peasants veer towards capitalism, 'poor' peasants are a 'rural proletariat in the process of formation' and 'middle' peasants have now been theorized out of existence into a worldwide category of 'petty commodity production'. Capitalism itself is so defined as to be virtually universal, and social formations are considered capitalist even if there is only a tiny proportion of capitalists and wage labourers in their work force:

> What makes enterprises, and more generally social formations, capitalist or not, is not their supposed essential features, *but the relations which structurally and historically explain their existence* (Gibbon and Neocosmos, 1985, p. 169; authors' emphasis).

Elsewhere, one of the participants in this debate has carried out painstaking and interesting work on the differentiation of an African peasantry (Neocosmos, 1987), and there is no doubt that the arguments are scholarly and well supported by references to

144

Marx, Lenin and other acceptable authorities. However, it is hard to escape the conclusion that the drive for conceptual purity has come to outweigh all other considerations. When we learn, for instance, that the Tanzanian state represents the petty-bourgeoisie, even though it is freely admitted that there is no petty-bourgeoisie in Tanzania, it should be evident that something is amiss. True, there are no 'facts' independent of 'theory', but there should be constraints on the way we indulge in theorizing. It all becomes quite futile if we allow the theoretical tail to wag the empirical dog.

## Summary

We have come a long way from the relatively slight attention paid to the Third World by classical Marxism. As indicated in the previous pages, and crudely and over-simplistically summarized in Figure 2, numerous strands have been interwoven in the production of world systems theory, which continues to be a crucial component in Marxist theories of underdevelopment. Marxist critics have argued that world systems theory is mistaken in its conceptualization of capitalism and modes of production and that it neglects the internal structures of Third World societies. At the heart of such criticisms are disagreements as to whether or not capitalist development is occurring in the Third World and how far it is possible to pinpoint the existence of indigenous bourgeoisies. Along with non-Marxists, some Marxists have argued that capitalist development is taking place and that, in some societies, indigenous industrialists are carrying out their allotted task and bringing about capitalist development, albeit unevenly, but nevertheless on similar lines to that which previously occurred in Western Europe. It has also been suggested that to depict the Third World as integrated into a comprehensive capitalist world system is to neglect the dynamic elements present in the formation of class relations and to minimize the importance of social action, thus reducing human actors to the status of puppets, more or less blindly acting out class roles according to their position within the world system. Culture, too, has become a dependent variable, merely mirroring economic and political dependence.

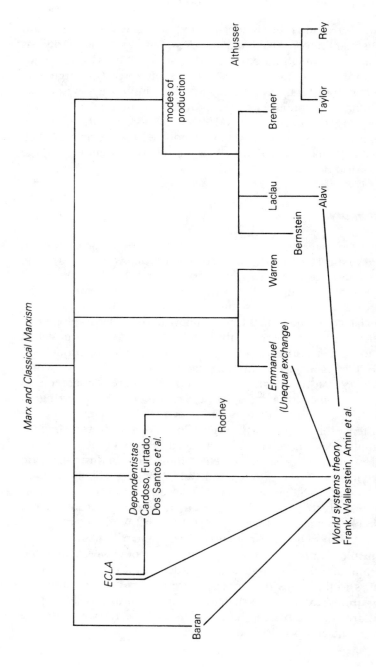

**Figure 2** The Development of Underdevelopment Theory

There have been numerous responses to world systems theory. Among Marxists some, for example, Cardoso, advocate a return to a more limited, more specific, more empirical examination of particular societies, with a renewed focus on their internal structures and the ways in which they are linked to the international economic environment. Nevertheless, it remains true that such structures continue to be 'conditioned' by their international situation. The Warrenites, too, advocate a more positive, empirical reassessment of Third World development, arguing that some economies, most notably those of the NICs, are being transformed along capitalist lines. The question of dependent capitalist development remains, but the focus is now on degrees of development and degrees of autonomy, rather than on dependency per se.

Concern with specific sectors of Third World economies, for example, Indian agriculture, has led to debate over the possible addition of new modes, or sub-modes, of production – colonial, post-colonial or peripheral – a discussion linked to the perceived need to review the nature of feudal and capitalist modes of production. At a different level, this need is also reflected in the 'articulations' controversy, where Third World social formations of the non-socialist variety are portrayed as distinctive, transitional structures, within which different modes of production, or their elements, articulate. According to this view, the economic, political and ideological spheres may all, at different times, possess a degree of 'relative autonomy', even though the economic sphere will be dominant 'in the last instance'. Despite its distinctive language and 'problematic', such an approach preserves, even develops, the concept of 'system', and may have more in common with earlier structural functionalist analysis than its proponents care to admit.

Finally, it has been shown that these debates have been reproduced in more geographically focused study of Third World regions and societies. They have been reproduced, but they have not been resolved, and it is clear that whilst world systems theory has prompted considerable discussion within underdevelopment theory, the latter is no more characterized by consensus than modernization theory. Indeed, the last two decades have perhaps demonstrated a need to return to themes once rejected out of hand as 'bourgeois', in order to arrive at a comprehensive framework for understanding the economic, political, social and cultural characteristics of Third World societies. If this is so, we may be faced with the (currently heretical) argument that modernization theory and underdevelopment theory are not mutually exclusive, incommensurable 'paradigms'. Could it be that some kind of synthesis is possible?

# 5
# Conclusions

*Modernization Theory and Underdevelopment Theory:*
*A Summary*

In the previous chapters, I have tried to show how major social scientific perspectives on the Third World have changed and developed, especially over the last four decades. Clearly, such an exercise involves considerable simplification.

In the years following the Second World War, modernization was generally accepted by social scientists, planners and politicians, both in the West and in the Third World. Although there were wide differences of opinion within this 'school', several themes and assumptions were shared by most of its adherents. The unit of analysis was usually the nation-state, and the nations of the Third World were placed on an evolutionary scale, at the apex of which were 'modern' Western societies. These provided a development pattern which, if followed in the Third World, would allow the 'developing' societies to catch up with the West, which was prepared to assist its (implicitly junior) partners by actively diffusing the ingredients necessary for development, especially 'modern' values, technology, expertise and capital. Within the Third World, the most active agents in the process of modernization were considered to be Western-educated elites, whose appointed task was to wean their people away from tradition and haul them, not without a degree of firmness, into the twentieth century.

It was the contrast of 'tradition' and 'modernity' which led some writers to refer to the dualism of Third World societies. The modern sector, industrial, capital-intensive and highly 'rational', was the leaven which would eventually transform the backward, traditional and mainly rural hinterland. Neo-evolutionism,

149

structural functionalism and diffusionism were the analytical frameworks which were taken from sociology and applied, often uncritically, to the Third World. In all of this, and throughout the sociology of the time, Talcott Parsons was the dominant figure. However, a word of caution bears repeating: simplification may be necessary but it does not justify caricature. Even at the end of the 1960s, while Parsons was developing his notion of the modern world system, strong criticisms were being expressed about his approach from within the modernization perspective. In the work of Barrington Moore and Bendix there was a stronger (and more empirical) emphasis on the socio-economic and political structures of specified industrializing societies, and Berger and his associates were applying the insights of phenomenological sociology to the modernization of the Third World. Even if we ignore the fact that, during this period, dependency theory was already a force in Latin America, it should be evident that at the beginning of the 1970s there was no unified sociology of development.

It could be argued that in classical Marxism we have a variant of modernization theory. By the end of the 1960s this orthodoxy was also being challenged. Numerous influences – ECLA and the dependentistas, the work of Baran as popularized and expanded by Frank, and contributions from other world systems theorists – were leading to a reassessment of classical Marxism and modernization theory. Again, a summary will necessarily be simplistic but several themes emerge. Development and underdevelopment are seen as opposite sides of the same process: development in one region occurs only at the expense of underdevelopment in another. Indeed, developed and underdeveloped societies participate in the same world system, which originated in capitalist expansion and colonialism. The system's parts are asymmetrically linked in a pattern of international trade which is characterized by 'unequal exchange'. According to this view, underdevelopment must be explained by reference to the structural position of Third World societies in the global economy and not, as in modernization theory, by the backwardness of their peoples or traditions, the lack of an educated elite, or by the absence of values considered to be conducive to (capitalist) development. True, some societies hitherto regarded as underdeveloped may have managed to climb out of the lowest category to become 'partially developed' in the 'semi-periphery', but their 'success', if it can be so described, has been achieved at the expense of other parts of the Third World. The plight of the Third World, which has arisen from participation in the world system, can be relieved only by the severance of such exploitative links. Underdeveloped societies must first become socialist and then 'go it alone', or develop alternative links with other genuine (and currently non-existing) socialist societies. This is the route they must follow to autonomous development, rather than vainly attempt to replicate the (alleged) history of capitalist development in the West.

The major tenets of underdevelopment theory seem to conflict directly with those of modernization theory, and mark (at the very least) a major change of emphasis in Marxist thinking. Indeed, I argued in the previous chapter that among the harshest critics of underdevelopment theory are Marxists who have quarrelled with its conception of capitalism and exploitation, or who have considered its focus on external linkages excessive and to detract from the necessary analysis of Third World social and political structures. To correct this imbalance, some theorists have tried to examine how specific Third World pre-capitalist modes of production 'articulate' with the dominant capitalist mode, whilst others have tried so to refine their concepts (for example, that of petty commodity production) that they are equally applicable to the Third World or the West. In addition, Marxist and non-Marxist alike have rejected the heuristic value of the notion of 'dependency', along with the empirical evidence that allegedly demonstrates the continued impoverishment of the Third World by the West. Instead, they have argued that capitalist development is occurring in the Third World, to the benefit of a wide range of its inhabitants and not merely the ruling or governing classes.

In passing, it is worth noting several similarities in these apparently distinct perspectives. First, they are all Eurocentric. They arise from within a body of thought firmly located in European experience, and they have been largely developed and applied by intellectuals, planners and politicians who have been socialized into this tradition. Secondly, like other notions of development, they embody a 'before' and an 'after', often with an implicit or explicit intermediate category. Modernization theorists tended to perceive the Third World from an evolution-ary position of presumed advantage and superiority: 'they' –

the backward or transitional societies – were on their way to becoming more like 'us'. By contrast, underdevelopment theory considers that the Third World should progress along a path towards a somewhat idealized (and socialist) version of what the West might have become, without the cruel intervention of capitalism. Even articulationists are not averse to referring to the transitional elements to be found in the articulation of pre-capitalist modes of production with the increasingly dominant capitalist mode. This is the language of change, of progress – in short, of development.

Thirdly, it is noteworthy that, in all the perspectives I have summarized, little attention is given to the views, wants, wishes and ambitions of those about to be developed. When they are taken into account it is often because they seem opposed to the grand designs of the 'objective' social scientist. The hapless actor is then categorized as 'falsely conscious', 'politically unaware' or 'traditional', the exact epithet depending on the position of the observer. This is not to imply that modernization theory and underdevelopment theory are unable to incorporate an action orientation, but they have usually focused more on 'macro' issues.

Finally, development theories of all kinds have been unable to ascribe a central position to gender relations. Lower-class aspirations have, in general, been neglected, but women's voices have been ignored more systematically than those of men. There are numerous reasons for this, including consistent structural inequality of women throughout the Third World (and not just the Third World) and a corresponding male bias on the part of theorists, planners and politicians, as well as at other social levels. However, some work has been done and it should not be underestimated. It was given recognition and added impetus with the declaration by the United Nations that 1975 to 1985 should be designated the 'International Decade for Women' and that 1975 should be 'International Women's Year'. As a result, attention was drawn to the problems of Third World women and their role in development, especially agriculture. Studies carried out from a modernization perspective examined the impact of education, industrialization and urbanization on women and their 'traditional' roles (cf. Nanda, 1976; Iglitzin and Ross, 1976). However, others have considered modernization theory to be inadequate: it has failed to see women as active, acting agents of development, and in practice the benefits brought to women by the processes of modernization have been illusory (Van Allen, 1976). Indeed, 'instead of eliminating patriarchy, it modernized it' (McCormack, 1981, p. 18). Arguably, Marxist theory has been no more success-ful. World systems theory and some articulationists have exam-ined the integral position of households in the production and reproduction necessary for the continuation of capitalism (Smith, Wallerstein and Evers, 1984). However, 'development studies remain firmly orientated towards men, men being synonymous with all people' (Rogers, 1980, p. 9). Dissatisfaction with Marxism has been a key factor in the growth of feminist social theory, in the West and elsewhere, and questions of patriarchy, of women's subordination, of family and household, of the sexual division of labour, and the problematic relationship between these questions and social class, are as relevant to the First and Second Worlds as to the Third (cf. Young, Wolkowitz and McCullagh, 1981). In this context, it is worth noting that, when compared with orthodox Marxists and underdevelopment theorists, feminists have been more even-handed in their criticisms; certainly, they are willing to focus on the continued exploitation of women in socialist as well as in capitalist societies.

## Modernization and Development

Views of 'development' are inevitably linked to some idea of progress, which involves a change, perhaps an evolution, from one state to another, both of which may be 'real' or idealized. The perspectives discussed in this book differ in their conceptions and evaluations of the directions in which the Third World is moving. Modernization theory emphasizes and approves of the trend towards Western, capitalist 'modernity', a view shared to some extent by orthodox Marxism, which prefers to regard capitalism as a necessary step on the path to socialism. Underdevelopment theory is more ambivalent: it denies capitalism can develop the Third World, primarily because it cannot reproduce the autonomous industrialization that allegedly occurred in the West. Instead, dependency must be short-circuited, exploitative links broken and socialism introduced, not just in one country but throughout the world system.

Disagreements about the nature of development are inevitably reflected in how 'it' should be measured. The focus of modernization theory on economic growth, per capita income, and such indices as literacy, access to medical services and the possession of consumer durables is clearly inadequate for underdevelopment theorists and many liberal critics. They do not reject growth as a feature, even a necessary feature, of development, but emphasize the additional requirement of central direction to ensure that basic needs are met and that there is an equitable share in the fruits of growth. This is at the heart of the current debate between the 'pro-marketeers' and those in favour of central planning. For the latter, there is no guaranteed 'trickle-down' effect and choices made within free market economies are insufficient to ensure justice for all.

The 'humanitarian' approach to development is nicely illustrated in the writing of Dudley Seers. In a paper now justifiably regarded as seminal, he argued that development involved 'the realisation of the potential of human personality' (1969, p. 2) and went on to suggest that this was best achieved through the reduction of poverty, unemployment and inequality. Alternatively, 'if one or two of these central problems have been growing worse, especially if all three have, it would be strange to call the result "development", even if per capita income doubled' (1969, p. 3). Asked to revisit his meaning of development, he felt it necessary to include self-reliance and increased cultural independence:

> development now implies, inter alia, reducing cultural dependence on one or more of the great powers – i.e. increasing the use of national language in schools, allotting more television time to programmes produced locally (or in neighbouring countries), raising the proportion of higher degrees obtained at home, etc (Seers, 1977, p. 5).

Clearly, there is no agreed definition of development. It is inescapably a normative term, which at various times has meant economic growth, structural economic change, autonomous industrialization, capitalism or socialism, self-actualization, and individual, national, regional and cultural self-reliance. In all of this, the distinction between means and ends can be lost. There is no reason to suppose, for example, that modernization theorists who see capitalist industrialization as the most effective path to development are any less sincere or moral in their concern for human welfare than underdevelopment theorists (and others) who emphasize equity in distribution and the satisfaction of basic needs. The two are not necessarily contradictory and to assert otherwise is to distort the debate. Nevertheless, it seems reasonable to regard development as a far-reaching, continuous and positively evaluated process of social, economic and political change which involves the totality of human experience. Individuals and collectivities will be affected, most dramatically, perhaps, in the Third World, and existing changes will be evaluated and measured according to the actors' and observers' standpoints. On really 'big' questions, such as the relative merits of socialism and capitalism, there will be lasting disagreement, but even here views have been known to alter. On other issues, perhaps of more immediate importance to those who are not social scientists, there may be a consensus. Few would regret the introduction of electricity to a village, for example, although opinion is likely to diverge with the consequent introduction of a juke box and numerous television sets.

By contrast, 'modernization' seems to be more easily defined. Put simply, 'modernity' is what is 'up-to-date' in a specific place at a given time. Generally, it will be an aspect of 'Westernization' involving changes which contrast with a previous 'traditional' stability. Indeed, any reference to modernity implies the juxtaposition of something new with a pre-established order. In such circumstances, conflict may occur, but it is not inevitable. Existing institutions can adapt, and the change may generally be acceptable. In addition, what is new may incorporate much of the traditional. To quote an example from the West: it is not easy to categorize the British monarchy. It can be regarded as modern, traditional, or a combination of both. At one extreme, what is modern might be a new fashion, a new form of dress or a different architectural style. Such apparently trivial change may nevertheless by imbued with deep cultural and religious significance and should not be dismissed lightly. Alternatively, modernization may also involve extensive structural changes. To take an example from Berger and his colleagues (Berger *et al.*, 1974), more comprehensive alterations in daily routines may follow the introduction of mass production: increased money incomes, changes in family structure, especially in the role of women, a decline in traditional handicraft production or in agriculture, and the pervasive influence of 'time-keeping', not only at work but also in other spheres of interaction. Such changes, operating in what Berger has recently described as 'an economic culture' (1987a, p. 7), are describable, verifiable and explainable, and they constitute a crucial area of sociological study.

What, then, is the difference between development and modernization? The former is a movement towards a valued state, which may or may not have been achieved in some other social context and which may not be achievable. The latter is a similar process. It is what is actually happening, for good or ill: a series of patterns with consequences that can be described, argued about and evaluated. If rated as good or 'progressive', the changes may be considered as a contribution to development, but they need not be evaluated in this manner. They may be seen as retrograde, as steps away from a desired state. In addition it is quite possible to be neutral. Many civil servants in West Africa, for example, wear 'Western' clothing at work and, when they return home, change into traditional dress. I find this neither progressive nor regressive; it is a small example of modernity, clearly describable and open to various interpretations. Others may wish to praise or condemn the practice. The basic point is that, positive, negative or neutral, there is no argument about what is happening. Much the same might be said of capitalism, a more comprehensive example of modernity. Despite the acrimonious debates over definitions, it is generally agreed that, ideal-typically, capitalism involves numerous well documented social processes: the separation of individual workers from their means of production, a corresponding increase in wage labour and participation in a cash economy, landlessness and (at least initially) increased inequality, production for profit, large-scale, capital-intensive manufacturing, the application of technology to production, and a vastly extended division of labour – all involving widespread and disruptive changes in the social, cultural, economic and political fabric of societies. The overall pattern is evident. The arguments are about how these interlinked processes should be evaluated. Do they amount to modernization or development?

## Sociology, Modernization and Development

Sociology has always been an eclectic social science, and there is no reason to suppose it will change in the foreseeable future. Its eclecticism lies partly in the fact that sociologists themselves adhere to different ideologies and have utilized a wide range of methodologies. There is no necessary connection between the two: neither structuralism nor functionalism, for example, are the exclusive preserve of any ideological faction, and the same can be said of action perspectives. Indeed, it is perhaps the divergences in sociological approaches that have prompted an almost continuous reflection on the nature of the discipline. In Britain, the 1970s commenced with a debate over 'The Two Sociologies' (Dawe, 1970), namely, systems theory and action theory, and drew to a close with a reformulation of the question as 'How Many Sociologies?' (Benton, 1978). Similar discussions have occurred elsewhere in the sociological universe, and the only fact that can be stated with any conviction is that we are no nearer agreement now than in the past. Interestingly, the central issue in the 'two sociologies' debate is the relationship between action theory and systems theory which highlights the distinction between the perceptions of acting subjects and the impersonal operation of social systems and social forces. In all sociology, including the study of modernization and development, it is necessary to examine 'objective' and measurable social processes as well as the 'subjective' and 'intersubjective' orientations of actors. Although individual sociologists will emphasize one or the other, the two approaches are complementary, and there is much in Benton's view that they are best understood 'as variant forms of one sociology' (1978, p. 218).

In a book such as this, it is (mercifully) no part of the writer's task to redraw the boundaries of sociology as a discipline. Irrespective of their ideologies and their theories, all sociologists are engaged in an attempt to understand the nature of society, the links across and within societies, and the rich variety of social action and interaction in which human beings participate. Whether their primary focus is on 'micro' or 'macro' elements of this interaction, sociologists continue to search for patterns which will help them describe, explain and make sense of the distinctive elements of social life with which they are confronted and in which they, too, are immersed.

In many respects, the founders of sociology provided the guidelines within which current debates about development are conducted. As previous chapters have demonstrated, their modern counterparts have frequently referred to the established 'classics' very much as religious leaders appeal to the prophets or sacred texts in support of their interpretation of social reality. Nevertheless, for the early theorists there was no common notion of development, except for the assumption – and assumption it normally remained – that the societies in which they were living had achieved development, or were well on the way to doing so. The early theorists were fascinated by, and sometimes frightened of the large-scale changes in economic and social structures they were witnessing and living through, and it was this fascination that led them to paint social change with such broad strokes. For most of them, social change and development were much the same thing. In this sense, and insofar as their concerns have been reflected by later sociologists, Goldthorpe is surely correct when he says that 'all sociology has been about "development", or whatever term is preferred' (1975, p. 7).

Like their modern (or traditional?) counterparts, the early sociologists were prompted to study society and search for underlying social patterns because society was apparently in a state of flux and, in trying to understand what 'makes society tick', they were also attempting to define their own position within it. Like us, they were conscious of, and perhaps obsessed by, the notion of 'modernity':

> To be modern is to experience personal and social life as a maelstrom, to find one's world and oneself in perpetual disintegration and renewal, trouble and anguish, ambiguity and contradiction: to be part of a universe in which all that is solid melts into the air. To be a modern*ist* is to make oneself somehow at home in the maelstrom, to make its rhythms one's own, to move within its currents in search of the forms of reality, of beauty, of freedom, of justice, that its fervid and perilous flow allows (Berman, 1983, pp. 345-6; author's emphasis).

Quite clearly, 'modernity' and 'development' are not only matters of concern in the Third World, as is indicated by the current intellectual preoccupation with 'modernism' and 'post-modernism' in the West. Like the poor, and by definition, modernity is always with us, and is preparing to make its contribution to tomorrow's tradition.

Because modernization and development are so closely linked, it makes sense to refer to the sociology of modernization and development. But if they are as closely connected as I have suggested, does this mean that sociology has moved full circle and there is no further point in concentrating on the Third World? After all, modernization and development are universal.

At one level, the question is irrelevant. Both modernization theory and underdevelopment theory have focused, in their different ways, on linkages of the constituent parts of the world system. Despite its concentration on the nation-state, modernization theory highlights the positive aspects of such connections, for example, the diffusion of values, cultures, technology, capital and expertise, whereas underdevelopment theory stresses the 'undesirable' elements and imbalance of the transfer or exchange. Similarly, the more theoretical and abstract examination of the articulation of modes of production (however many there happen to be), and the corresponding search for concepts that can be applied 'across the board', indicate that the study of modernization and development will never be confined to nation-states alone. Indeed, it has recently been argued that the growth of the nation-state was, in any case, part and parcel of the expansion of the world system. With the increase in the industrial and military strength of Europe, its consequent colonization of the Third World, and the expansion of state power backed by military force, the existence and autonomy of the modern nation-state was brought into being, and increasingly monitored by international organizations:

'International relations' are not connections set up between pre-established states, which could maintain their sovereign power without them: they are the basis upon which the nation-state exists at all. The period of the burgeoning of international organizations, including the League of Nations and the U.N., is not one of the growing transcendence of the nation-state. It is one in which the universal scope of the nation-state was established (Giddens, 1985, pp. 263-4).

In effect, the development of the 'world system' and the growth of the nation-state went together.

Giddens also argues that, at least in one respect, the concept of the Third World is redundant:

> With the exception of the diffusion of nuclear weapons... virtually all modern states are 'First World' in one sense – they possess the material and organizational means of waging industrialized war (Giddens, 1985, p. 293).

This may be so, but it should also be evident that the degree to which states can sustain such wars, and the levels of technology they can bring to bear, vary enormously across the world system. In any case, to assert that, at one level, the world is one is not to demonstrate a unity in other spheres of activity.

Paradoxically, some world systems theorists are inclined to question the usefulness of the concept of a Third World, but distinguish societies that are capitalist (or firmly entrenched in the capitalist periphery) from those following a political path that can be broadly defined as socialist. By this token, Cuba and Jamaica, or Ethiopia and Chad, are clearly in different camps, whereas in other respects they may be directly comparable. This 'two world' approach can be contrasted with Frank's insistence that the countries of the Eastern bloc are being incorporated into the capitalist world system, as consumers and producers – a view which points to the increasing possibility of a sociology of the world! (cf. Frank, 1980, pp. 256-62).

The 'two worlds' view of capitalism and socialism also seems to have drawn support from a very different quarter. It has been asserted that Third World countries are so heterogeneous, economically, culturally and in virtually every other way, that they exhibit no single defining feature – except, perhaps, the desire for and receipt of aid: 'The concept of the Third World and the policy of official aid are inseparable. The one would not exist without the other' (Bauer, 1984, p. 40).

Against such views, it is commonly held that the concept of a 'Third World' is both meaningful and useful. According to Horowitz, it refers to a 'self-defined and self-conscious association of nation states' (1972, p. 17), characterized by the following features:

First, it tends to be politically independent of both power centers, the United States – NATO complex and the Soviet Warsaw-Pact group. Second, the bulk of the Third World was in a colonial condition until World War II. Third, it draws its technology from the First World while drawing its ideology from the Second World. Thus, the Third World is non-American, ex-colonial, and thoroughly dedicated to becoming industrialized, whatever the economic costs (Horowitz, 1972, pp. 16-17).

That there are problems with this kind of definition is hardly surprising, given its level of generality. Nevertheless, there is a large measure of agreement among social scientists of different theoretical persuasions, and among ordinary people, as to what constitutes the Third World (or the South, developing, underdeveloped or peripheral societies). The countries on every list would be much the same. The Third World is an abstraction, a form of shorthand which denotes a collection of colonies, ex-colonies and nation-states broadly distinguished from the First World of the United States and its allies and the Second World of the USSR and the Eastern bloc by a variety of economic, political and social criteria. Economically, such states typically have low GNPs, high rates of unemployment and underemployment, high levels of absolute poverty, starvation and malnutrition, and non-industrial economies which normally rely on the export of primary products in international markets dominated by Western capitalism. Most Third World states obtained political independence after the Second World War and are defined, at least by their leaders, as non-aligned. Their social structures are typically inegalitarian, with relatively small middle and upper classes (insofar as these can be distinguished) and a high proportion of agriculturalists, often described as peasants. The upper classes retain political power, as much through coercion and the control of the armed forces as by consensus, and there are usually wide variations in culture and ethnicity among the lower classes, and between them and their rulers.

Clearly, Third World societies are heterogeneous and will vary considerably in the extent to which they reveal the above characteristics. In addition, it is possible to identify some features in regions of the First World (cf. Seers, 1977, p. 6), as well as in the Second. Some Third World societies are very wealthy, for example, Kuwait and Saudi Arabia, and most parts of the First World will fall below them in terms of per capita incomes. It has to be recognized that there will always be anomalies in bringing a disparate collection of societies under one category. However, these 'objective' features constitute an ideal type, an abstraction from reality, which can be useful in comparing one society, or group of societies, with another. It is a heuristic device which is intended to facilitate sociological analysis, and not to function as a conceptual straight jacket (cf. Weber, 1949, pp. 89-104). In short, those who find the notion of the Third World unhelpful are at liberty to dispense with it or to use alternative concepts. My guess is that it will be demonstrably useful for a long time to come, and that those who avoid it will probably have to replace it with a similar concept. One further remark on this topic: it is abundantly clear, but not always mentioned, that another common feature of Third World societies is that most of their members are non-Caucasian, whereas most citizens of the First and Second Worlds are phenotypically white. When this is added to the perceived ills of colonialism and neo-colonialism, we are faced with a mix which, subjectively as well as objectively, amounts to yet another deep division in the world system. As Toye remarks,

> The Third World is not... yet able to be dismissed from our minds. It is not a figment of our imagination ready to vanish when we blink. It is a result of our collective lack of imagination, our inability in our present difficult circumstances yet to see ourselves as belonging to one world, and not three (1987, p. 10).

To summarize: the sociology of modernization and development is that branch of sociology which examines the processes of modernization and development, especially but not exclusively in the Third World, where they are most evident and dramatic. As part of this project, it is necessary to study domestic social, political and economic structures, as well as their continued linkages with external institutions, societies and systems. In all of this, the most specific concern of sociology is with social relations and social processes and their economic, political and cultural connotations.

## *The Problem of Paradigms*

The study of internal structures should not be put forward as an alternative to a focus on linkages of the component parts of the world system. We are not dealing with an either-or dilemma, where blame must be attributed to indigenous people or outside interference. But internal and external 'variables' will rarely be of equal importance. Clearly, there are countless examples of the immense effect of colonialism, trade or direct invasion on specific societies or regions. Nevertheless, it should also be evident that the nature of domestic social, cultural, political and economic institutions will have a crucial bearing on the processes of modernization and development. Apart from anything else, they help determine how social change will be instigated, accepted, rejected, acted upon, acted out or altered by indigenous people. Crude arguments that see class structures or cultures as pale reflections of metropolitan interests do less than justice to the vibrant variety of cultures that is found in the Third World. In effect, they brand whole nations, and sometimes the working class in metropolitan countries, as cultural dupes. Similarly, insofar as modernization theorists concentrated on the nation-state (a charge of which some, at least, are palpably innocent) they have ignored key features of modernization and development. And theorists of all persuasions have often failed to recognize the ability of actors to bring about change, individually and collectively, even in the face of overwhelming odds.

Such comments may appear banal. However, in the heady days of the 1970s it was commonplace to refer to modernization theory and underdevelopment theory as separate 'paradigms', and to the increased dominance of the latter as an example of 'paradigm shift' (Foster-Carter, 1976). Such a tendency is still evident (cf. Blomstrom and Hettne, 1984, pp. 2-4 and p. 197), and given the subsequent disillusionment many have experienced with underdevelopment theory, this is even more misplaced.

The notion of paradigm arises from the world of Kuhn (1970a and 1970b). He opposes the conventional wisdom that, in the natural sciences, knowledge accumulates gradually, much in the same way that a tower might be constructed from individual bricks. Instead, scientific progress, as defined by members of the scientific community, occurs in fits and starts, with extended periods of 'normal' scientific activity punctuated by crises which may, in certain conditions, lead to radical changes in the dominant perspective. Kuhn portrays this route to 'normal science' as passing through four stages. First, there is a non-guided, more or less random collection of facts, which leads into the second, pre-paradigm stage, where 'schools' compete with one another to have their view of a discipline, and their interpretations of data, accepted by others. At the third stage, one paradigm triumphs and this, in turn, leads to the stage of normal science, which is characterized by a general acceptance of an underlying world view, its associated norms and values and its methods of solving puzzles. The rules behind the methods are rarely explicit or, indeed, explicable: they are intuited and internalized by novices as part of their socialization into the discipline. And when allegiances change, it is not because there has been a convincing proof or a conclusive logical argument, but because there has been a radical shift in the scientists' world view. They undergo 'a conversion experience' (Kuhn, 1970a, p. 151).

There are numerous problems associated with Kuhn's treatment of normal science, not all of which are relevant here. It is a moot point, for example, whether or not the natural sciences have developed in the way he describes (cf. Suppe, 1977). In addition, he is inconsistent in his definition of paradigms. Initially, the term was applied to the entire spectrum of beliefs of a scientific community, ranging from metaphysics to the rules underlying research methods. Later, it was virtually abandoned and Kuhn referred, instead, to the 'disciplinary matrix' of a community and its 'exemplars'. The former denotes the general consensus in a community over common symbolic generalizations and particular norms and values. More narrowly, exemplars are paradigms in the restricted sense of established models of problem solving. However, Kuhn was consistent in arguing that what ultimately distinguishes one paradigm from another is their incommensurability: it is impossible to translate the language of one into the language of the other. In the absence of a neutral language, the only way a member of one group can really understand the theories of another is to become a convert, to change his or her world view and look at the world through new eyes.

In discussing the relevance of Kuhn's concept of paradigms to the sociology of modernization and development, three questions must be asked: first, is sociology a science substantially akin to the natural sciences? Secondly, does it have a prevailing 'normal science' and any likely competitors? Thirdly, if a positive response can be given to these questions, are such paradigms also found in the sociology of modernization and development?

On the first question, few sociologists are prepared to argue, these days, that sociology can emulate the natural sciences and most would regard the attempt as undesirable. Many sociologists have claimed to be scientific, but there was, and is, little agreement as what this claim actually means. If in doubt, compare Marx, Durkheim and Weber, not to mention their successors. If it is acknowledged that the social interaction studied by many sociologists is the (possibly unintended) outcome of actions taken by human subjects of their own volition, sociology immediately parts company with the natural sciences. For Marx and Weber, certainly, purposeful social action was a key feature, and even Durkheim, in his attempt to establish sociology as a science, nevertheless regarded societies as moral systems. In fact, many sociologists would deny sociology any scientific status, and perhaps as many more would consider the question irrelevant. Of course, it is regularly claimed that sociology can and should emulate the natural sciences in the rigour, replicability and 'objectivity' of their methods, to the extent that there is a 'unity of method', but that is not the present issue. When faced with the relationship of sociology to natural science the only answer that emerges from the community of sociologists is that, at the very least, there is no agreement. And if this is the case, Kuhn's concept of paradigm is inapplicable to sociology.

It then becomes somewhat academic to ask if there is a 'normal science' within sociology. However, even supporters of the notion of paradigm-shift recognize that the answer to this question is negative. Although different centres of sociology may be noted for their adherence to particular perspectives, it is impossible to isolate a dominant paradigm, let alone a 'normal science'. Within the discipline, even within departments, there are numerous cross-cutting tensions: between Marxists and non-Marxists, among Marxists, between action perspectives and systems theory, and so on. None of these can be regarded as dominant. Even if we could accept that sociology and the natural sciences were comparable, in a Kuhnian sense, sociology could have progressed only as far as the 'pre-paradigm' stage en route to normal science. One possible response to this is to focus on the narrower definition of paradigm – the exemplar, the model approach to problem solving. It would then become necessary to show 'at least one area of research that is guided by concrete examples of scholarship, which serve to generate and solve puzzles' (Eckberg and Hill, 1979, p. 935). No such exemplars exist in sociology.

In a sense, the third question has been made redundant. If there are no sociological paradigms, they can hardly be transferred into the sociology of modernization and development, which is but the application of standard sociological perspectives to a specific area of concern. In any event, it is difficult to isolate contenders for paradigm status: modernization theory (whose?) against Marxism? Whose Marxism? Not everyone agrees that underdevelopment theory is Marxist, (cf. Foster-Carter, 1979), and some Marxists clearly have much in common with modernization theory. Underdevelopment theory versus modernization theory? Both contain strong functionalist elements and, even in general sociology, functionalism and its opponents are not paradigms; they are not: 'widely recognized achievements which practically and conceptually define the course of future research' (Eckberg and Hill, 1979, p. 930).

On balance, it seems best to abandon the notions of paradigm and paradigm-shift when referring to competing perspectives in the sociology of modernization and development. Indeed, 'competing perspectives' neatly summarizes the framework of the debate: the idea of a perspective implies a partial view of a particular event, a view which may or may not coincide with that of another participant or observer. Anyone attempting to understand the event in question requires accounts from as many perspectives as possible, and even the most 'reliable' of witnesses may have a different story to tell. Perhaps the analogy should not be pushed too far. Nevertheless, this approach is similar to Weber's conception of social science. There is no universal social scientific truth, valid for all time, but a focus on a 'finite portion of reality' which we have defined in advance as 'culturally significant', or 'worthy of being known'. Inevitably, the knowledge we obtain will be partial and validated. It will be partial because every perspective will illuminate different aspects of reality, and it will be validated, or capable of validation, from within the community of scholars, who are themselves situated in a cultural context which defines their area of study – in this instance, modernization and development – as culturally significant (cf. Weber, 1949, pp. 71-113). As Weber remarks, 'All knowledge of cultural reality, as may be seen, is always knowledge from *particular points of view*' (1949, p. 81; author's emphasis).

## *The Commensurability of Perspectives*

The sociology of modernization and development, which focuses on social change, especially in the Third World, and how it is interpreted, is made up of a variety of perspectives. They are not mutually exclusive, however much their proponents claim privileged access to the truth. As the previous chapters demonstrate, there has been continuous debate about the relative importance of a whole range of 'variables' influencing modernization and development. Arguments have occurred over the degree to which Third World problems are caused by endogenous, as opposed to exogenous, influences. Has development been facilitated or reversed by overseas investment? How crucial are indigenous social, political and economic structures in the process of change? What role do cultures play in aiding, blocking, or even defining 'development'? What is the effect of centralized state planning on the trajectory of Third World societies? The fact that these discussions occur, and that positions are altered, is an indication that we are not talking of mutually exclusive language groups who cannot communicate with one another. Sometimes the dialogue is direct, as between Platt and the Steins over the role of overseas investment in Latin America (as described in the previous chapter), or between Safford and Berquist on the relative importance of values, geography and economic and social structures in the formation of a technical elite in Columbia (cf. Berquist, 1978; Safford, 1978). Ironically, the latter exchange, 'On Paradigms and the Pursuit of the Practical', clearly indicates the practicability of useful discussion across perspectives and the inappropriateness of the concept of paradigms in this context.

Positions often change for the simple reason that new empirical evidence makes a previous stance untenable. In recent years, the role of the state as a prime mover in planning social change has been under attack, both theoretically and politically. In China, Eastern Europe and in parts of the Third World, including Tanzania, as well as within international organizations such as the World Bank, it is now recognized that state planning is no guarantee of success as measured in terms of industrialization and national income. Indeed, at times it may be counter-productive. Academically, the attack has come from the so-called New Right (more appropriately, the Liberal Revival) which has argued that central planning in the Third World (and elsewhere) has led already inefficient and perhaps corrupt governments to interfere with free trade, with disastrous results. Stretched to carry out even the 'essential functions' of government, they have failed: 'They often seem anxious to plan but are unable to govern' (Bauer, 1984, p. 28). All too often, they accept 'the apparatus, symbols and rhetoric of planning' (Little, 1982, p. 56), but lack the discipline and forethought to carry it through. Not all involved in this liberal revival are totally opposed to state planning, but there is a consensus that it should be greatly reduced and confined mainly to oiling the wheels of the market. Indeed, it is said that the most important lesson to be learned from Third World economic performance over the last three decades is that 'efficient growth which raises the demand for unskilled labour by "getting the prices right" is probably the single most important means of alleviating poverty' (Lal, 1983, p. 102).

Some attacks on the 'developmental state' have evoked a sympathetic response from 'the Left'. It is agreed that much Third World planning has been inefficient, with bureaucrats as inclined to line their (private) pockets as to pursue the public good. This has long been known. It is also recognized that many government agencies and para-statals have actually made matters worse. Commenting on Nigerian marketing boards, for instance, Williams concludes: 'Against such corrupt institutions and monopolistic arrangements, socialists should support free trade' (1985, p. 13). However, opponents of the 'counter-revolution also point to the fact that the Newly Industrialising Countries so beloved of the free marketeers do not support their case. In South Korea and Taiwan, the empirical evidence points to substantial and continuous state involvement at all levels (Wade and White, 1984). In addition, it is noted that opponents of state planning say little about national and transnational monopolies, which also operate against the principles of free trade. If such principles are to be upheld, the state must interfere so that the market can operate, and thus it is incorrect to regard the roles of the market and the state as necessarily in conflict. And to argue that one has not succeeded is not a sufficient justification for emphasizing the other. As Toye remarks, 'the ploy of using government failure to outweigh that of market failure is a shallow one' (1987, p. 66).

My basic point in this discussion is not that one side is right and the other wrong but that once again we are being presented with a false choice.

> Until we recognise that the problem will not be solved until the right kind of politics is in command, we will continue to replace one set of inadequate policies with another equally lacking in conviction (Brett, 1987, p. 37).

Quite what Brett means by 'the right kind of politics' is unclear, but if this line is followed we are forced to examine the empirical evidence of what is happening in the Third World, especially in the NICs. The emphasis will be on the political sphere, thus returning us to the concerns of Bendix and Barrington Moore (as outlined in Chapter 2) as well as to some of the dependency theorists.

In other areas of debate, too, the necessity to return to the empirical evidence is being realized. Among Marxists, for example, there has been considerable discussion of the nature of Kenyan capitalism, with some suggesting that local capital is subservient to international capital and others attributing a more independent role to the former. As part of the 'Kenya debate', there is also disagreement on the importance of the peasantry, or sections of it, in the spread of capitalism. The issues have been admirably summarized by Kitching, (1985) and I have no wish, or space, to reproduce them here. However, it is noteworthy that he concludes that whilst empirical data can clearly be interpreted differently from different positions, 'these *are* questions which to a degree are empirically resolvable' (1985, p. 140; author's emphasis). Even more importantly, he declares that among radicals there has been such a widespread loss of faith that, at present, there is hardly any 'practically available' alternative to capitalism in Africa:

The cause of this 'crisis of radical belief' is not hard to discern. It lies in the widely recognized (but rarely publically acknowledged) fact that *all* of the various 'socialist' experiments and regimes in black Africa to date have at best had ambiguous results for the welfare of the peasants and workers who live under them, and at worst have been an unambiguous disaster (Kitching, 1985, pp. 144-5; author's emphasis).

As it happens, I agree with Kitching, both in his depiction of radical disillusionment and (sadly) in the implication that it is justified. But that is not the point. What is absolutely crucial, though, is that such a conclusion has been reached by many social scientists on the basis of the available empirical evidence, *even though they did not want to believe it*. Had we really been talking about paradigms in the Kuhnian sense, this would not have been possible.

Seen in this light, other quarrels might be regarded as less bleak and stark. To give a final example, some of the deepest rifts have been over the role of the transnational companies in the Third World. Putting the matter crudely, modernization theorists have considered them to be engines of development, useful in the diffusion of capital, technology, expertise and 'modern' attitudes, and in the creation of employment, whereas underdevelopment theorists have usually branded them agents of neo-colonialism, exploiting the masses of the Third World, expropriating capital, encouraging the brain drain, actively disrupting local crafts and industry, and generally reinforcing underdevelopment. However, this is not a straightforward argument between Marxists and non-Marxists: the Warrenite position on transnationals is more circumspect and others, too, are prepared to credit transnationals with a role in development (Emmanuel, 1982). Once we leave the generalizations behind, the position is by no means clear. Much depends on the type of product – processed manufacture, primary foodstuff or mineral – and whether it is for export or domestic consumption. The size of the transnational and the extent of its world operations, as well as the nature of its links with the society in question, must also be considered, as should that country's culture and social, political and economic structures. Links of the 'host' society with others in the region, with international 'blocs' of producers, perhaps through the United Nations or with one or more of the

'Big Powers', also influence the nature of its relationship with the transnational company. Once such matters are raised, the extent of 'diffusion' from the transnational and 'expropriation' from the Third World become more empirical issues. The two perspectives are not mutually exclusive, and they have been jointly applied to a study of transnational companies in Nigeria. The author of this study concludes,

> The only way that both theoretical and policy-relevant knowledge is going to progress on the controversial issues of international political economy is through the dialectical confrontation of alternative theoretical perspectives (Biersteker, 1978, pp. 160-1).

It is perhaps worth mentioning that Biersteker, on balance, comes down in favour of the greater usefulness of underdevelopment theory in studying the Nigerian context, but he clearly favours the dual approach. This is no assertion that we are faced with 'incompatible world views and a consequently unbridgeable communications gap' (Foster-Carter, 1976, p. 176). Rather, it is a recognition that, despite competing ideologies and divergent definitions of development, there is a limited commensurability across perspectives. In the end, there is a common approach to empirical data. This is not to suggest that the facts 'speak for themselves', but that the parameters to these arguments have already been set – by a Western intellectual tradition of social analysis within which Marx, Durkheim, Weber and all their heirs are firmly located.

That there are differences in terminology cannot be doubted. Such terms as ruling class, elite, governing class and bourgeoisie are situated in competing perspectives. Sometimes they can replace one another with little or no loss of meaning; at other times they may embody more of an alternative stance towards empirical reality, but at no time do they represent alternative realities.

I have argued for limited commensurability across perspectives, a common recognition of what constitutes empirical evidence and, even among those who eschew 'empiricism', the shared inheritance of a Western intellectual tradition. Clearly, this is not to suggest that commensurability is complete. Linked to and underlying the perspectives described in this book are values and ideologies which are deeply held. In effect, these ideologies, which often centre on the desirability or otherwise of capitalism or socialism, involve prior definitions of development. It has to be emphasized that it is not idiosyncratic for social scientists in general, or sociologists in particular, to adhere to beliefs which are embedded in their social and cultural environment; for them, as for others, they constitute lived ideologies into which they are socialized and according to which they evaluate a whole range of social scientific and other data. Invariably, too, there will be divisions within social science arising from the selection and examination of some aspect of cultural reality by people with different beliefs. In this sense, there is no such thing as a 'value-free' sociology and I know of no one (least of all Weber) who has claimed that such a sociology should exist. Indeed, ideological differences largely explain the intensity of the debates described in the previous chapters of this book. That people do shift position remains the case, but it is often only after a considerable degree of heart-searching and weighing evidence which goes against the ideological grain.

In my view, which is clearly not without its ideological aspects, it is quite justifiable to indicate the ideological position which implicitly or explicitly frames an academic argument. Toye can thus legitimately remark of Bauer's objections to government planning that

> his categories are the politicization of economic life, the centralization of political power, corruption and the erosion of economic and political freedom. All of these essentially political considerations sum up to the evils of totalitarianism, although the word itself has much less salience in his current vocabulary than it did in his vocabulary of the 1950s (Toye, 1987, p. 64).

But, as Toye recognizes, to indicate an ideological position is not to refute (or prove) an argument. By the same token, sociologists should not dismiss the work on markets of Hayek, a key figure on the 'New Right', simply because he approvingly quotes a police view that 'a noticeable proportion of today's terrorists have studied sociology or political or educational sciences' (1978,

p. 29). At an ideological level, not even economists are immune from quoting nonsense. Furthermore, this kind of mistake is not the prerogative of 'the Right'. On 'the Left' there is at least as great a willingness to confuse ideology and social science. At a well attended seminar, when two respected ('Left wing') academics had presented a paper on a World Bank report, suggesting that it might have something to recommend it, the first question they had to field was 'Whose side are you on?' Following the correct political ideology was apparently more important than empirical evidence and careful academic inquiry, and to agree with the World Bank on anything was to betray the cause. Or consider this gem, from the writer of a highly competent history of Jamaica:

> If anyone classified by me as bourgeois feels offended and would like to be regarded as a Marxist, or at least radical, let them appeal to the highest of all courts, their role in the struggle for socialism. No doubt they will find me there, pleading my own case (Post, 1978, p. 475).

At a less ludicrous level, numerous examples could be given of a tendency to parade a 'Left' position: the dedications to unknown heroes of the revolution, the disparaging remarks about 'unpopular' politicians, and the pretence or illusion that by producing an academic text the revolution of the masses is being advanced. Indeed, the history of underdevelopment theory illustrates an unfortunate association with this kind of politicization. It undoubtedly highlighted Third World links with metropolitan powers, and continues to produce valuable empirical studies and theoretical insights. But it was also 'dysfunctional' in that it enabled many academics and politicians to focus almost entirely on externalities and to neglect, or regard as unimportant, what was happening within Third World societies. The exogenous became a substitute for, and not a complement to, the endogenous. As a result, the recent awareness in underdevelopment theory that renewed attention must be paid to Third World structures has led, for some, to disillusionment. The promise of the new 'paradigm' to the young of the Third World has been broken; the 'radical supervisors' who offered such attractive socialist alternatives have betrayed their trust; not only have they neglected international capitalism, the 'main enemy', but also they have dared to criticize

African leaders (Gurnah, 1985). Such disillusionment has occurred because political ideology has been too closely linked with socio- logical theory and research, and when the latter are scrutinized and revised, the former seems to have been betrayed.

'Liberals', too, may attribute the status of separate paradigms to approaches to development different from their own. Chambers (1986) refers to ('top-down') 'normal professionalism' as core- centred, specialized, quantitative and technocratic, and to ('bottom- up') 'new professionalism' as periphery- and people-centred, flexible, qualitative and non-bureaucratic. This draws attention to the role of international organizations in socializing politicians, planners and other developmentalists into a particular, organiz- ation-based, institutionalized perception of development, but it also implies a new version of 'us' and 'them', with the warm, the concerned, the carers ('us') on one side and the cold, calculating, rational and technocratic ('them') on the other. In fact, employees of international organizations may be as concerned with the plight of the poor as freelance consultants and will thus resent the slur cast upon them by such 'keepers of morality' (cf. Conlin, 1985, p. 84). If there are 'goodies' and 'baddies' in the world of modernization and development, they cannot be so neatly categorized.

In fact, there is genuine disagreement within and across perspectives as to what development is and how it should be achieved. Across the spectrum, many would accept that, ultimately, they are talking about autonomous industrialization, insofar as this is, or ever was, possible – certainly as a means to an end and occasionally even as an end in itself. However, there will be a divergence as to whether this should be along capitalist or socialist lines, at least in the first instance, and over which of these 'paths' is best able to satisfy the basic needs of the poor. That said, 'bottom up' and 'top down' policies have no natural affiliation with any perspective, and an examination of policies on specific 'problems' reveals numerous examples of unlikely allies. Both 'Left' (Hayter, 1981; Hayter and Watson, 1985) and 'Right' (Bauer, 1984), for totally different reasons, reject bilateral and multilateral aid as being of any value to the Third World, while Hayek echoes many on the Left who argue that population growth does not work against productivity increases, except when it is subsidized by the state (1983, p. 52). Indeed, as I suggested earlier, the role of the state in the Third World is currently being assessed across the political divides. In addition, there is no agreed policy on urbanization: it is largely ignored or considered secondary by underdevelopment theory, given a variety of labels by the articulationists and regarded, somewhat passively, as an index of development by modernization theory. Similarly, the Right and the Left are equally contemptuous of the idea that the plight of rural areas can be much eased by piecemeal reform. Ultimately, in fact, such terms and 'Left' and 'Right' are quite meaningless when it comes to making sense of development policy. It may then be a council of despair to assert that social change in the Third World must be left, so to speak, to the working class, or that only Third World leaders have the right to determine national policies.

## Continuing Themes in the Sociology of Modernization and Development

My interpretation of the sociology of modernization and development incorporates modernization theory, underdevelopment theory and other perspectives, but lacks the grandiose claims sometimes made on their behalf. No all-embracing view of the Third World, or world system, is on offer, and none is on the horizon. True, new models of development can be found in the Third World: Cuba, Tanzania, China and other socialist hopefuls no longer fire the imagination but such capitalist societies as Taiwan, Hong Kong and South Korea are now portrayed as examples for others to follow. They, too, should be treated with caution. Sociologists who set themselves up as prophets of some new order, and tie their sociology to a political ideology, do their discipline no service. It behoves them, instead, to examine processes of social change in the Third World, and the ways in which they are acted out, acted upon and interpreted with care, attention, and not a little scepticism. This is a substantial challenge, and the theoretical perspectives outlined in the previous pages undoubtedly provide frameworks for this continuing project. The questions will vary with the theoretical and ideological predilictions of individual sociologists, and with the focus of their empirical research, but the answers will be subject to review by their peers, including those of other persuasions, according to the accepted canons of sociological inquiry. In fact, behind the rhetoric, this is very much what happens wherever social scientists gather to discuss issues of modernization and development in the Third World.

From previous chapters of this book, some important themes emerge which are relevant in the study of modernization and development. First, there is the perpetual tension between individual actors and the social systems which they themselves have constituted. As Dawe makes clear (1979), this dichotomy has been a feature of all major sociological perspectives. People are actively involved in making their own history; they are purposeful actors. Yet the results of their actions are not necessarily of their own choosing; they are constrained within all kinds of socially produced cages. This is as true in the Third World as elsewhere, and it is inevitably reflected in the sociology of modernization and development when the 'systemic' elements of social life are studied at all levels, from world systems, regions, nation-states, social classes, religious and ethnic groups to such primary groups as families and households. Clearly, in all of this, the role of social anthropology is crucial and can only be separated artificially from sociology. And other disciplines will also contribute: history, geography, economics, international relations, and so on. As we have seen, sociological emphases will vary, but no one perspective has exclusive access to reality. All views are partial.

Secondly, the continuing process of industrialization, capitalist or socialist, is a clear example of modernization and, for many, a key feature of development. In all perspectives, it occupies a major place and will continue to do so. The nature of industrialization, its accompanying features, and the degree to which they are inevitable, will remain at the centre of the agenda. In this context, it would be useful if more studies comparing socialist industrialization with that of capitalism were undertaken.

Thirdly, and following from this, we cannot dispose of culture. Culture can be defined in hundreds of ways, every one of which will be disputed. Attempts are made to deconstitute it or reconstitute it, always from 'outside', and it may be subsumed as 'ideology', with or without disparaging connotations. Simplistically, though, what people learn in their social context about production and government, and the nature of their beliefs, values and social

176

mores, cannot be dismissed as some kind of derivative variable, ultimately resting on an economic 'base'.

As Worsley remarks, 'the concept of culture has been virtually ignored by those social scientists who reduce the study of society to political economy or the study of social structure' (1984, p. 41). And as the preceding pages demonstrate, the study of culture has been significantly absent since the demise of modernization theory, except perhaps in the United States, where underdevelopment theory has met more of a sustained challenge from the previously dominant perspective. Culture is not a matter of mere beliefs, even though these are important; rather, it 'has three dimensions: the *cognitive*, the *normative* and the *conative* (Worsley, 1984, p. 42; author's emphasis). In effect, cultures provide us with cognitive maps, by reference to which we can situate ourselves in the world, intellectually, mentally, psychologically and socially. They offer institutionalized frameworks of evaluation, enabling 'us' to distinguish ourselves from 'them', and they also constitute ready-made, but perhaps competing, sets of instructions about how we should behave.

Modernization theorists can be criticized for a naive, 'clipboard' approach to values and culture, where personality types and cultural characteristics are derived from a study of questionnaire responses. Attempts at such categorization are not necessarily buried in the past (cf. Hofstede, 1984). However, to ignore culture almost completely is no less an error, and yet we are close enough to this situation for Worsley to refer to culture as 'the missing concept' (1984, p. 41). This is not quite correct: the notion of 'cultural imperialism', whilst unfortunately implying a hierarchy of cultures, some of which are stronger than others, nevertheless drew attention to collective perceptions and their links with external influences. Clearly, culture should not be studied in isolation. There is much to recommend Berger's concept of 'economic culture', which refers to the 'social, political and cultural matrix or context within which... particular economic processes operate' (1987a, p. 7), but what is more important than any label is to avoid predetermining the direction of causality.

What we need to avoid is not only the assumption that the 'cultural' is a *separate* sphere, but that is is causally *secondary* (merely 'super-structural'). It is, in fact, the realm of those crucial institutions in which the ideas we live by are produced and through which they are communicated – and penetrate even the economy (Worsley, 1984, p. 60).

Interestingly, the revival of interest in 'the market' in the First, Second and Third Worlds requires us to ask how choices are determined in the first place. What people eat, drink and choose to purchase, sell or exchange is rarely, if ever, a matter of economic necessity alone. As Sahlins remarks,

> Marx spends much time in *Capital* explaining why a certain quantity of wheat is equivalent in value to x hundredweight of iron. While the answer to the rate of equivalence in terms of average necessary social labour is surely brilliant, it does not tell us why wheat and why iron; why certain commodities are produced and exchanged and not others (1976, p. 149).

In short, economic behaviour is always situated within a cultural context.

Sometimes the 'New Right' returns us to a more direct focus on culture, and one which is reminiscent of early modernization theory. Having argued that 'firm but limited government' in the colonies allowed the 'illiterate peasantry' of South-east Asia and West Africa to use their entrepreneurial talents, Bauer goes on to suggest that culture is responsible for variations in economic performance. Group differences, among which he includes ethnicity, are crucial, and conventional economic evidence on land-person ratios and capital is misleading. 'The small size and low productivity of so many farms in the Third World primarily reflect want of ambition, energy, skill, and not want of land or capital' (Bauer, 1984, p. 8). Hayek, too, justifies the spread of 'commercial morality' and the corresponding and necessary decline of a more primitive 'altruism' by noting that certain rules concerning property and family life were stumbled upon by some groups, who then 'prospered and multiplied more than others' (Hayek, 1983, p. 47). By the end of the eighteenth century, these values had spread throughout the West, and were socialized into succeeding generations for as long as small enterprise was dominant. However, it was not because of superior intelligence or deliberate choice that such values were accepted: 'It was a process of cultural selection, which made those groups and their practices prevail' (Hayek, 1983, p. 47).

It is ironic that, in the 1980s, a position so politically influential in the West appears to be legitimated by recourse to so crude a version of modernization theory – and this from someone who thinks so little of sociology. Nevertheless, it would be inappropriate if, as a consequence, we were to ignore the work of the 'New Right' on markets. In addition, and more importantly, we do not have to agree with Bauer or Hayek before we place cultures and values at the centre of the development debate. To deny them any standing in the sociology of modernization and development is to assert that what people think, believe and act upon is of no consequence, a position which, for any sociologist, is surely untenable. Apart from anything else, it is the people themselves, in their various nations, classes and groups, who bring to the processes of social change their own evaluations of what is good and bad about industrialization and other forms of modernization. They, too, have ideas about what constitutes development, and we must beware of selecting as their 'representatives' only those whose political ideology may coincide with our own. As Foster-Carter remarks, our knowledge of them can be gained only 'via a dialogue *with* their knowledge and [must] indeed be fashioned out of their knowledge' (1987, p. 223; author's emphasis). Here, perhaps, the sociologist's need of the anthropologist is at its greatest, and the sooner a common cause is realized the better it will be for the study of modernization and development.

Fourthly, it is clear that sociology must focus on both 'objective' and 'subjective' features of development. Both are 'worth being known' and, although individual sociologists may prefer to emphasize one or the other, they are not exclusive concerns. Whilst it is important to 'bring the actors back' into the study of modernization and development, it is equally necessary to observe and try to explain the social, economic and cultural contexts in which they operate, always remembering that such 'objectivity' will be from a specific vantage point.

Fifthly, the linked concepts of diffusion and innovation should be revived. Indeed, they were never completely laid to rest, and the idea of cultural imperialism is the equivalent of cultural diffusion, albeit from a more critical angle. Nevertheless, although the simplistic notion that Western values or capital inevitably bring great benefits is clearly inadequate, the opposite assumption, that the transfer is necessarily pernicious, is equally false. Values, beliefs, tastes, priorities and items of trade are obviously transferred, and the process is usually two-way. The degree of symmetry will vary from one situation to another, and to some extent it can be demonstrated empirically, but the fact remains that such transfers occur. Over the last decade, they have often been ignored, except by those examining the implications of technical change, and it is time that sociologists again attended to such matters. They could do worse than start with themselves, for social scientists in Western institutions have played a key role in diffusing Western ideas to the Third World. And they continue to do so. The very people who reject the concept of diffusion as bourgeois and ideological are actively involved, in their teaching, their writing and perhaps in their work as consultants, in disseminating Western ideology and ideas. If proof were needed, the history of modernization theory, underdevelopment theory, all other forms of Marxism (with the possible exception of Maoism) and feminist theory can readily be cited. Indeed, as I suggested earlier, the growth of development studies itself is deeply rooted in Western intellectual and political thought.

Important though academics imagine themselves to be, their influence is unlikely to match that of the international bureaucrat, who perhaps received his or her training in Europe or North America. In this context, the United Nations is the socializing agency par excellence. Ordinary citizens may not participate in the process, but their representatives are socialized into development-oriented ways of thinking, and into all the conflicting perceptions this entails. In part, this is what Chambers (1986) refers to as 'normal professionalism' (even though Chambers, too, is a professional developmentalist). We may argue about the effectiveness of the United Nations and its component organizations, or about the validity of its 'collective' approach to development (if it exists), but it provides a crucial venue for the diffusion of ideas which are subsequently found all over the world. More than this, the United Nations provides for their increased dissemination. In other words, international organizations and national bodies in the Third World to which they are linked are key actors in the diffusion of ideas, capital, technologies, expertise, and so on. It is also worth paying attention to the careers of prominent individuals within such organizations as the World Bank, and the extent to which they exert influence not only as technocrats but also as academics and political advisers. Clearly, they can be regarded as epitomizing the interlinkages of technocratic, bureaucratic and political interests which are so vital in international relations and in the spread of 'information' across national boundaries.

At a lower level, the network of diffusers is linked to formal and informal education systems throughout the Third World, and the role of the mass media is vital. Few sociologists will deny the importance of such linkages. Although they may offer different evaluations of what is taught – the 'baddies' inculcate ideology or practise brainwashing, and the 'goodies' transmit knowledge or raise consciousness – the importance of the activity is not in doubt. It reaches to the lowest primary groups – families, households and peer groups – and they, in turn, carry out their own socialization and reinforce the process, simultaneously altering and interpreting the information, values and priorities which they are receiving from such a variety of sources.

Finally, sociologists should return, again, to political structures and the nature of political leadership. This is not to argue that economic structures should be neglected but to argue for an alteration in balance. In particular, it cannot be assumed that the economic sphere is dominant, even in the last instance, for it is well known that the last instance never comes. In a sense, this process is already under way: underdevelopment theory has recognized the need for a more specific focus on the political sphere and Seers, too, recommends that we examine 'the motivation, will power, judgement and intelligence of actual or potential leaders' (1981a, p. 11). I am tempted to add that, given their Western counterparts, they should not be assessed too harshly. Nevertheless, such injunctions return us to the concerns of Bendix and Barrington Moore. But the focus should not only be on 'the elite' or the 'ruling class'; we must also follow underdevelopment theory in studying their connections with institutions and groups outside their own society. In addition, it is worth examining how they 'articulate' with members of their own ethnic groups and societies, and the extent to which government is based on the consensus of the people. Repression is not the exclusive property of any political system. Indeed, an examination of the military in the Third World, their position in the social and economic structure, nationally and internationally, is long overdue.

I have suggested several themes that are central in the sociology of modernization and development: the actor and the system; industrialization, culture, values and economic change; diffusion and innovation; and the importance of political structures. They are but a selection, and all involve a recognition that studies of internal and external units, and their interlinkages, are complementary. This view of the discipline is eclectic and partial. Despite the existence among sociologists, as among others, of deep ideological differences over the nature of capitalism, socialism and development, dialogue does occur, and even here positions are changed, albeit with great reluctance. At a lower level, there is agreement over how empirical evidence should be treated and debates are common, often prompting reassessment in substantive areas of research. It is for this reason that I refer not to paradigms but to a limited commensurability across perspectives. Indeed, according to Held, this is an accurate reflection of the state of general sociology, at least in Britain:

> Some of the major innovations in sociology in the past decade have been linked to systematic developments in social theory which have led to the reconstruction of sociology and its tasks. The highly polemical exchanges, for example, between advocates of 'Marxist' and 'mainstream' sociology, characteristic of the late 1960s and 1970s, have come to an end. The upshot has been a theoretical enrichment of sociology. While there has not been a total convergence between Marxist and mainstream sociologies, the most contemporary sociology bears the mark of a variety of theoretical perspectives and has built upon a clear understanding of the limitations of previous paradigms. The result is certainly increased theoretical sophistication and a greater willingness to use this sophistication to *illuminate problem-orientated research* (Held, 1987, p. 4).

Paradigms we may not have, but no one is pretending that the sociology of modernization and development lacks disputes or that it is characterized by gentle and unassuming consensus. Even those who share similar ideologies are not averse to engaging in internecine warfare. But no one should expect sociology to bring happiness. As Weber remarks, 'Who believes in this? Aside from a few big children in university chairs or editorial offices' (1948, p. 143). Nevertheless, sociologists who study the Third World and its relations with the First and Second Worlds are engaged in a common project, and share the belief that modernization and development can be described, understood and at least sometimes explained. This does not seem an unreasonable or unworthy aim, and it is certainly consistent with a genuine desire to alleviate hunger and suffering in the Third World. Many would regard it as a precondition for success in such a venture.

Given the stakes, it is to be expected that ideologies will differ, and the debates will be fierce and long. Nevertheless, it is perhaps worth remembering that 'in the lecture-rooms of the university no other virtue holds but plain intellectual integrity' (Weber, 1948, p. 156).

# Bibliography

Alavi, H. (1975), 'India and the colonial mode of production', in R. Miliband and J. Savile (eds), *The Socialist Register* (London: Merlin), pp. 160-97.

Alavi, H. (1983), 'Colonial and post-colonial societies', in T. B. Bottomore, L. Harris, V. G. Kiernan and R. Miliband (eds), *A Dictionary of Marxist Thought* (Oxford: Blackwell), pp. 81-2.

Amin, S. (1974), 'Accumulation and development: a theoretical model', *Review of African Political Economy*, no. 1, August-November, pp. 9-26.

Amin, S. (1976), *Unequal Development: An Essay on the Social Formulation of Peripheral Capitalism* (Hassocks: Harvester).

Angell, N. (1910), *The Great Illusion: A Study of the Relation of Military Power in Nations to their Economic and Social Advantage* (London: Heinemann).

Arensberg, C. M. and Kimball, S. T. (1968), *Family and Community in Ireland*, 2nd edition (Cambridge, Mass.: Harvard University Press). First published in 1940 (Cambridge, Mass.: Harvard University Press).

Baran, P. (1973), *The Political Economy of Growth*, with an introduction by R. B. Sutcliffe (Harmondsworth: Penguin). First published in 1957 (New York: *Monthly Review Press*).

Barratt Brown, M. (1972), 'A critique of Marxist theories of imperialism' in R. Owen and B. Sutcliffe (eds), *Studies in the Theory of Imperialism* (London: Longman), pp. 35-70.

Bauer, p. (1984), *Reality and Rhetoric: Studies in the Economics of Development* (London: Weidenfeld & Nicolson).

Bendix, R. (1964), *Nation-Building and Citizenship: Studies of Our Changing Social Order* (New York and London: Wiley).

Bendix, R. (1966), 'A case study in cultural and educational mobility: Japan and the protestant ethic', in N. J. Smelser and S. M. Lipset (eds), *Social Structure and Mobility in Economic Development* (Chicago, Ill.: Aldine), pp. 262-79).

Bendix, R. (1967), 'Tradition and modernity reconsidered', *Comparative Studies in Society and History*, IX, (3), pp. 292-346.

Benton, T. (1978), 'How many sociologies?' *Sociological Review*, 26, (2), May, pp. 217-36.

Berger, P. (1977), *Pyramids of Sacrifice* (Harmondsworth: Penguin).

Berger, P. (1987a), *The Capitalist Revolution: Fifty Propositions About Prosperity, Equality and Liberty* (Aldershot: Gower).

Berger, P. (1987b), *Modern Capitalism, Vol. II: Capitalism and Equality in the Third World* (Boston, Mass.: Hamilton Press).

Berger, P., Berger, B., and Kellner, H. (1974), *The Homeless Mind* (Harmondsworth: Penguin).

Berger, P., and Luckmann, T. (1967), *The Social Construction of Reality* (Harmondsworth: Penguin).

Berman, M. (1983), *All That is Solid Melts Into Air: The Experience of Modernity* (London: Verso).

Bernstein, H. (1971), 'Modernization theory and the sociological study of development', *Journal of Development Studies*, 7, (2), January, pp. 141-60.

Bernstein, H. (ed) (1976), *Underdevelopment and Development: The Third World Today*, 2nd edition (Harmondsworth: Penguin).

Bernstein, H. (1977), 'Notes on capital and peasantry', *Review of African Political Economy*, No. 10, September/December, pp. 60-73.

Bernstein, H. (1979), 'Sociology of underdevelopment vs. sociology of development?' in D. Lehmann (ed.), *Development Theory: Four Critical Studies* (London: Cass), pp. 77-106.

Bernstein, H. (1981), 'Notes on state and peasantry: The Tanzanian case', *Review of African Political Economy*, No. 21, May/September, pp. 44-62.

Bernstein, H. (1987), 'Of virtuous peasants', in T. Shanin (ed.), *Peasants and Peasant Societies*, 2nd edition (Oxford: Blackwell), pp. 449-51.

Berquist, C. W. (1978), 'On paradigms and the pursuit of the practical', *Latin American Research Review, XIII*, (2), pp. 247-51.

Biersteker, T. J. (1978), *Distortion or Development? Contending Perspectives on the Multinational Corporations* (London: MIT Press).

Blomstrom, M. and Hettne, B. (1984), *Development Theory in Transition: The Dependency Debate and Beyond: Third World Responses* (London: Zed Books).

Bock, K. (1964), 'Theories of progress and evolution' in W. Cahnman and A. Boskoff (eds), *Sociology and History: Theory and Research* (New York: Free Press), pp. 21-41.

Bock, K. (1979), 'Theories of progress, development, evolution', in T. B. Bottomore and R. Nisbet, (eds), *A History of Sociological Analysis* (London: Heinemann), pp. 39-79.

Booth, D. (1975), 'Andre Gunder Frank: an introduction and appreciation', in I. Oxaal, T. Barnett and D. Booth, (eds), *Beyond the Sociology of Development* (London: Routledge & Kegan Paul), pp. 50-86.

Bradby, B. (1975), 'The destruction of natural economy', *Economy and Society*, vol. 4, pp. 125-61.

Brenner, R. (1977), 'The origins of capitalist development: a critique of neo-Smithian Marxism', *New Left Review*, no. 104, July/August, pp. 27-92.

Brett, E. A. (1987), 'States, markets and private power in the developing world: problems and possibilities', in J. Dearlove and G. White (eds), *IDS Bulletin* (Sussex: Institute of Development Studies), 18, (3), July, pp. 31-7.

Brewer, A. (1980), *Marxist Theories of Imperialism: A Critical Survey* (London: Routledge & Kegan Paul).

Cardoso, F. H. (1977), 'The consumption of dependency theory in the United States', *Latin American Research Review*, XII, (3), pp. 7-24.

Chambers, R. (1986), 'Normal professionalism, new paradigms and development', *Discussion Paper*, no. 227 (Sussex: Institute of Development Studies).

Cliffe, L. and Lawrence, P. (1977), 'Editorial', *Review of African Political Economy*, no. 8, January-April, pp. 1-6.

Cohen, R. (1980), 'Resistance and hidden forms of consciousness among African workers', *Review of African Political Economy*, no. 19, September–December, pp. 8-22.

Conlin, S. (1985), 'Anthropological advice in a Government context', in R. Grillo and A. Rew (eds), *Social Anthropology and Development Policy* (London and New York: Tavistock), pp. 73-87.

Cruise O'Brien, D. (1979), 'Modernization, order, and the erosion of a democratic ideal: American political science 1960-1970', in D. Lehmann (ed.), *Development Theory: Four Critical Studies* (London: Cass), pp. 49-76.

Dawe, A. (1970), 'The two sociologies', *British Journal of Sociology*, XII, (2), pp. 207-18.

Dawe, A. (1979), 'Theories of social action', in T. B. Bottomore and R. Nisbet (eds), *A History of Sociological Analysis* (London: Heinemann), pp. 362-417.

Dore, R. P. (1977) 'Underdevelopment in theoretical perspective', *Discussion Paper*, no. 109 (Sussex: Institute of Development Studies).

Dos Santos, T. (1970), 'The structure of dependence', *American Economic Review*, 60, (2), pp. 231-6.

Dos Santos, T. (1976), 'The crisis of development theory and the problem of dependence in Latin America', in H. Bernstein (ed.), *Underdevelopment and Development: The Third World Today*, 2nd edition (Harmondsworth: Penguin), pp. 57-80.

Durkheim, E. (1964), *The Division of Labour in Society* (New York: Free Press).

Durkheim, E. (1982), *The Rules of Sociological Method and Selected Texts on Sociology and its Method*, edited and with an Introduction by S. Lukes (London: Macmillan).

Eckberg, D. L., and Hill, L. (1979), 'The paradigm concept and sociology: a critical review', *American Sociological Review*, vol. 44, December, pp. 925-37.

Eisenstadt, S. N. (1964), 'Social change, differentiation and evolution', *American Sociological Review*, 29, (3), June, pp. 375-86.

Eisenstadt, S. N. (1966), *Modernization, Protest and Change*

(Englewood Cliffs, N. J.: Prentice-Hall).

Eisenstadt, S. N. (1968), *Comparative Perspectives on Social Change* (Boston, Mass.: Little, Brown & Co).

Eisenstadt, S. N. (1970), 'Social change and development' in S. N. Eisenstadt (ed.), *Readings in Social Evolution and Development* (Oxford: Pergamon), pp. 3-33.

Emmanuel, A. (1972), *Unequal Exchange: A Study in the Imperialism of Trade* (New York and London: Monthly Review Press).

Emmanuel, A. (1982), *Appropriate or Underdeveloped Technology* (Chichester: John Wiley).

Erikson, E. H. (1950), *Childhood and Society* (New York: Norton).

Etzioni-Halevy, E. (1981), *Social Change: The Advent and Maturation of Modern Society* (London: Routledge & Kegan Paul).

Evans-Pritchard, E. (1962), *Essays in Social Anthropology* (London: Faber & Faber).

Foster, G. (1962), *Traditional Cultures and the Impact of Technological Change* (New York: Harper & Row).

Foster, G. (1965), 'Peasant society and the image of limited good', *American Anthropologist*, vol. 67, pp. 293-315.

Foster-Carter, A. (1976), 'From Rostow to Gunder Frank: conflicting paradigms in the analysis of underdevelopment', *World Development*, 4, (3), March, pp. 167-80.

Foster-Carter, A. (1978), 'Can we articulate "articulation"?' in J. Clammer (ed.), *The New Economic Anthropology* (London: Macmillan), pp. 210-49.

Foster-Carter, A. (1979), 'Marxism versus dependency theory? A polemic', *Occasional Papers*, No. 8, University of Leeds.

Foster-Carter, A. (1987), 'Knowing what they mean: or why is there no phenomenology in the sociology of development?', in J. Clammer (ed.), *Beyond the New Economic Anthropology* (London: Macmillan), pp. 202-29.

Frank, A. G. (1969), *Latin America: Underdevelopment or Revolution?* (New York and London: Monthly Review Press).

Frank, A. G. (1972), *Lumpenbourgeoisie: Lumpendevelopment – Dependence, Class and Politics in Latin America* (New York and London: Monthly Review Press).

Frank, A. G. (1975), 'A disclaimer', *Latin American Research Perspectives*, Issue 4, Spring, II, (1), pp. 65-6.

Frank, A. G. (1976), 'Rebuttal', *Latin American Perspectives*, Issue 9, Spring, III, (2), pp. 106-7.

Frank, A. G. (1978), *Dependent Accumulation and Underdevelopment* (London: Macmillan).

Frank, A. G. (1980), *Crisis: In the World Economy* (London: Heinemann).

von Freyhold, M. (1977), 'The post-colonial state and its Tanzanian version', *Review of African Political Economy*, no. 8, January-April, 1977, pp. 75-89.

Frölich, P. (1972), *Rosa Luxemburg* (London: Pluto Press).

Gibbon, P., and Neocosmos, M. (1985), 'Some problems in the political economy of "African socialism"', in H. Bernstein and B. K. Campbell (eds), *Contradictions of Accumulation in Africa: Studies in Economy and State* (Beverly Hills, Ca.: Sage), pp. 153-206.

Giddens, A. (1985), *A Contemporary Critique of Historical Materialism, Vol. II: The Nation-State and Violence* (London: Polity).

Goldthorpe, J. E. (1975), *The Sociology of the Third World* (Cambridge: Cambridge University Press).

Goodman, D., and Redclift, R. (1981), *From Peasant to Proletarian: Capitalist Development and Agrarian Transitions* (Oxford: Blackwell).

Gouldner, A. W. (1971), *The Coming Crisis of Western Sociology* (London: Heinemann).

Green, R. (ed.) (1973), *Protestantism, Capitalism and Social Science: The Weber Thesis Controversy* (Boston, Mass.: Heath).

Gurnah, A. (1985), 'Whither paradigm?', *Review of African Political Economy*, no. 32, April, pp. 116-20.

Hagen, E. (1962), *On the Theory of Social Change* (Homewood, Ill.: Dorsey Press).

Harrison, D. (1975), 'Social relations in a Trinidadian village', Ph.D. thesis, University of London.

Hayek, F. A. (1978) *The Three Sources of Human Values* (London: The London School of Economics and Political Science).

Hayek, F. (1983), *Knowledge, Evolution and Society* (London: Adam Smith Institute).

Hayter, T. (1981), *The Creation of World Poverty: An Alternative to the Brandt Report* (London: Pluto Press).

Hayter, T., and Watson, C. (1985), *Aid: Rhetoric and Reality* (London: Pluto Press).

Held, D. (1987), 'The future of sociology', *Network*, Newsletter of the British Sociological Association, no. 39, October, pp. 3-6.

Herskovits, M., and Herskovits, F. (1947), *Trinidad Village* (New York: Knopf).

Higgott, R. (1978), 'Competing theoretical perspectives on development and underdevelopment: a recent intellectual history', *Politics*, XIII, May, pp. 26-41.

Hobsbawm, E. (1964), 'Introduction to K. Marx', *Pre-Capitalist Economic Formations* (London: Lawrence & Wishart) pp. 9-65.

Hobsbawm, E. J. (1979), 'The development of the world economy', *Cambridge Journal of Economics*, 3, (3), September, pp. 305-18.

Hobson, J. A. (1902), *Imperialism: A Study* (London: Allen & Unwin).

Hofstede, G. (1984), *Culture's Consequences: International Differences in Work-Related Values* (Beverly Hills, Ca.: Sage).

Hoogvelt, A. (1976), *The Sociology of Developing Societies* (London: Macmillan).

Horowitz, I. L. (1972), *Three Worlds of Development: The Theory and Practice of International Stratification*, 2nd Edition (London: Oxford University Press).

Hoselitz, B. (ed.) (1952), *The Progress of Underdeveloped Areas* (Chicago, Ill.: University of Chicago Press).

Hoselitz, B. (1960), *Sociological Aspects of Economic Growth* (New York: Free Press).

Iglitzin, L. B., and Ross, R. (eds) (1976), *Women in the World: A Comparative Study* (Santa Barbara, Ca. and Oxford: Clio Books).

Inkeles, A., and Smith, D. H. (1974), *Becoming Modern* (Cambridge, Mass.: Harvard University Press).

Kahn, J. S., and Llobera, J. R. (1981), 'Towards a new Marxism or a new anthropology?', in J. S. Kahn and J. R. Llobera (eds), *The Anthropology of Precapitalist Societies* (London: Macmillan), pp. 264-324.

Kiernan, V. G. (1974), *Marxism and Imperialism* (London: Edward Arnold).

Kitching, G. (1985), 'Politics, method and evidence in the "Kenya" debate', in H. Bernstein and B. K. Campbell (eds), *Contradictions of Accumulation in Africa: Studies in Economy and State* (Beverly Hills, Ca.: Sage), pp. 115-51.

Kuhn, T. S. (1970a), *The Structure of Scientific Revolutions*, 2nd Edition (Chicago, Ill.: University of Chicago Press).

Kuhn, T. S. (1970b), 'Reflections on my critics', in I. Lakatos and A. Musgrave (eds), *Criticism and the Growth of Knowledge* (Cambridge: Cambridge University Press), pp. 231-78.

Laclau, E. (1979), *Politics and Ideology in Marxist Theory* (London: Verso).

Lal, D. (1983), *The Poverty of Development Economics* (London: The Institute of Economic Affairs).

Leaf, M. J. (1979), *Man, Mind and Science: A History of Anthropology* (New York: Columbia University Press).

Lenin, V. I. (1965), *Imperialism, The Highest Stage of Capitalism* (Peking: Foreign Languages Press).

Lerner, D. (1958), *The Passing of Traditional Society* (New York: Free Press).

Levitt, K. (1968), 'Dependence and disintegration in Canada', *New World Quarterly*, IV, (2), pp. 57-139.

Levy, M. J. (1952a), 'Some sources of the vulnerability of the structures of relatively non-industrialized societies to those of highly industrialized societies', in B. F. Hoselitz (ed.), *The Progress of Underdeveloped Areas* (Chicago, Ill.: University of Chicago Press), pp. 113-25.

Levy, M. J. (1952b), *The Structure of Society* (Princeton, N.J.: Princeton University Press).

Levy, M. J. (1966), *Modernization and the Structure of Societies*, Vols. I and II (Princeton, N.J.: Princeton University Press).

Lewis, O. (1966), 'The culture of poverty', *The Scientific American*, 215, (4), October, pp. 19-25.

Leys, C. (1975), *Underdevelopment in Kenya: The Political Economy of Neo-Colonialism* (London: Heinemann).

Leys, C. (1976), 'The "over-developed" post-colonial state: a re-evaluation', *Review of African Political Economy*, no. 5, January-April, pp. 39-48.

Leys, C. (1977), 'Underdevelopment and dependency: critical notes', *Journal of Contemporary Asia*, 7 (1), pp. 92-107.

Leys, C. (1978), 'Capital accumulation, class formation and dependency – the Significance of the Kenyan case', *The Socialist Register*, pp. 241-66.

Leys, C. (1980), 'Kenya: what does "dependency" explain?', *Review of African Political Economy*, no. 17, January-April, pp. 108-13.

Lipset, S. M. (1967), 'Values, education and entrepreneurship', in S. M. Lipset and A. Solari (eds), *Elites in Latin America* (New York: Oxford University Press), pp. 3-60.

Little, I. M. D. (1982), *Economic Development: Theory, Policy, and International Relations* (New York: Basic Books).

Luxemburg, R. (1951), *The Accumulation of Capital*, with an Introduction by Joan Robinson (London: Routledge).

Mahleka, A. (1976), 'Comments on Nsari', *Review of African Political Economy*, no. 6, May-August, pp. 81-4.

Mandel, E. (1978), *Late Capitalism* (London: Verso).

Marshall, G. (1982) *In Search of the Spirit of Capitalism* (London: Hutchinson).

Marx, K. (1954), *Capital*, Vol. I. (London: Lawrence & Wishart).

Marx, K. (1959), *Capital*, Vol. III. (London: Lawrence & Wishart).

McClelland, D. C. (1976), *The Achieving Society* (New York: Van Nostrand. First published in 1961 (New York: Free Press).

McCormack, T. (1981), 'Development with equity for women', in N. Black and A. Baker Cottrell (eds), *Women and World Change: Equity Issues in Development* (Beverly Hills, Ca.: Sage), pp. 15-30.

Melotti, U. (1977), *Marx and the Third World* (London: Macmillan).

Mommsen, W. (1981), *Theories of Imperialism* (London: Weidenfeld & Nicolson).

Moore, Barrington (1967), *Social Origins of Dictatorship and Democracy: Lord and Peasant in the Making of the Modern World* (Harmondsworth: Penguin).

Moore, W. E. (1964), 'Predicting discontinuities in social change', *American Sociological Review*, 29, (3), pp. 331-8.

Moore, W. E. (1979), 'Functionalism' in T. B. Bottomore and R. Nisbet (eds), *A History of Sociological Analysis* (London: Heinemann), pp. 321-61.

Nanda, B. R. (ed.) (1976), *Indian Women From Purdah to Modernity* (New Delhi: Vikas).

Neocosmos, M. (ed.) (1987), *Social Relations in Rural Swaziland: A Critical Analysis* (Swaziland: Social Science Research Unit, University of Swaziland).

Ness, G. D., Shapiro, G. and Hobsbawm, E. J. (1967), 'Review symposium: Barrington Moore, social origins of dictatorship and democracy', *American Sociological Review*, 32, (5), October, pp. 818-22.

Nettl, J. P. (1966), *Rosa Luxemburg* (London: Oxford University Press).

Nisbet, R. (1966), *The Sociological Tradition* (New York: Basic Books).

Ohlin, G. (1970), 'The evolution of aid doctrine', in J. Bhagwati and R. S. Eckans (eds), *Foreign Aid* (Harmondsworth: Penguin), pp. 21-62.

Palma, G. (1978), 'Dependency: a formal theory of underdevelopment or a methodology for the analysis of concrete situations of underdevelopment?', *World Development*, 6, (7/8), pp. 881-924.

Parsons, T. (1951), *The Social System* (Glencoe, Ill.: Free Press).

Parsons, T. (1957), 'Malinowski and the Theory of Social Systems', in R. Firth (ed.), *Man and Culture: An Evaluation of the Work of Bronislaw Malinowski* (London: Routledge & Kegan Paul), pp. 53-70.

Parsons, T. (1964), 'Evolutionary universals in society', *American Sociological Review*, 29, (3), June, pp. 339-57.

Parsons, T. (1966), *Societies: Evolutionary and Comparative Perspectives* (Englewood Cliffs, N.J.: Prentice-Hall).

Parsons, T. (1971), *The System of Modern Societies* (Englewood Cliffs, N.J.: Prentice-Hall).

Parsons, T., and Shils, E. (eds) (1962), *Towards a General Theory of Action* (New York: Harper & Row).

Petras, J. (1978), *Critical Perspectives on Imperialism and Social Class in the Third World* (New York and London: Monthly Review Press).

Phillips, A. (1977), 'The concept of development', *Review of African Political Economy*, no. 8, January-April, pp. 7-20.

Platt, D. C. M. (1980a), 'Dependency in nineteenth-century America: an historian objects', *Latin American Research Review*, XV, (1), pp. 113-20.

Platt, D. C. M. (1980b), 'The anatomy of "autonomy" (whatever that may mean)', *Latin American Research Review*, XV, (1), pp. 147-9.

Poggi, G. (1968), 'Social origins of dictatorship and democracy', *British Journal of Sociology*, vol. 19, pp. 215-17.

Post, K. (1978), *Arise Ye Starvelings: The Jamaican Labour Rebellion of 1938 and its Aftermath* (The Hague: Martinus Nijhoff).

Randolph, L. I., and Randolph, S. H. (1967), *The Modernity of Tradition* (Chicago, Ill.: University of Chicago Press).

Ray, D. (1973), 'The dependency model of Latin American underdevelopment: three basic fallacies', *Journal of Inter-American Studies*, 15, (1), February, pp. 4-20.

Riggs, F. W. (1964), *Administration in Developing Countries: The Theory of Prismatic Society* (Boston, Mass.: Houghton Mifflin).

Rodney, W. (1972), *How Europe Underdeveloped Africa* (London: Bogle-L'Ouverture).

Rogers, B. (1980), *The Domestication of Women: Discrimination in Developing Societies* (London: Kogan Page).

Rogers, E. M. (1962), *Diffusion of Innovations* (New York: Free Press).

Rostow, W. W. (1960) *The Stages of Economic Growth: A Non-Communist Manifesto* (London: Cambridge University Press). Reference is also made to the second (1971) edition (London: Cambridge University Press).

Rostow, W. W. (ed.) (1963), *The Economics of Take-off into Sustained Growth*, Proceedings of a conference held by the International Economic Association (London: Macmillan).

Rostow, W. W. (1978), *The World Economy: History and Prospect* (London: Macmillan).

Ruccio, D. F. and Simon, L. H. (1986), 'Methodological aspects of a Marxian approach to development: an analysis of the modes of production school', *World Development*, 14, (2), pp. 211-22.

Safford, F. (1978), 'On paradigms and the pursuit of the practical: a response', *Latin American Research Review*, XIII, (2), pp. 252-60.

Sahlins, M. (1976), *Culture and Practical Reason* (Chicago, Ill.: University of Chicago Press).

Seers, D. (1969), 'The meaning of development', *International Development Review*, 11, (4), pp. 2-6.

Seers, D. (1977), 'The new meaning of development', *International Development Review*, 19, (3), pp. 2-7.

Seers, D. (1981a), 'Development options: the strengths and weaknesses of dependency theories in explaining a government's room to manoeuvre', *Discussion Paper*, no. 165 (Sussex: Institute of Development Studies).

Seers, D. (ed.) (1981b), *Dependency Theory: A Critical Reassessment* (London: Pinter).

Sender, J., and Smith, S. (1986), *The Development of Capitalism in Africa* (London: Methuen).

Shivji, I. (1975), 'Peasants and class alliances', *Review of African Political Economy*, no. 3, May-September, pp. 10-18.

Smelser, N. J. (1969), 'Mechanisms of and adjustments to change', in T. Burns (ed.), *Industrial Man* (Harmondsworth: Penguin), pp. 43-68.

Smith, J., Wallerstein, I. and Evers, H. (eds) (1984), *Explorations in the World-Economy, Vol. 3: Households and the World Economy* (Beverly Hills, Ca.: Sage).

Smith, M. G. (1965), *The Plural Society in the British West Indies* (Berkeley, Ca.: University of California Press).

Smith, M. G. (1966), 'Pre-industrial stratification systems', in N. J. Smelser and S. M. Lipset (eds), *Social Structure and Mobility in Economic Development* (Chicago, Ill.: Aldine) pp. 141-76.

Smith, M. G. (1974), *Corporations and Society* (Duckworth: London).

Smith, S. (1983), 'Class analysis versus world system: critique of Samir Amin's typololgy of development', in P. Limqueco and B. McFarlane (eds), *Neo-Marxist Theories of Development* (London: Croom Helm), pp. 73-86.

Solo, R. A., and Rogers, E. M. (eds) (1972), *Including Technological Change for Economic Growth and Development* (Michigan: Michigan State University Press).

Spengler, J.J. (1955), 'Social structure, state, economic growth', in S. Kuznets, W. E. Moore and J. J. Spengler (eds), *Economic Growth: Brazil, India, Japan* (Durham, N.C.: Duke University Press), pp. 363-87.

Srinivas, M. N. (1962), *Caste in Modern India* (London: J. K. Publishers).

Stanton, R. (1975), 'Talking about consciousness', in D. Seers (ed.), 'CULTURAL dependence?' *Bulletin* (Sussex: Institute of Development Studies), 7, (1), April, pp. 36-9.

Stein, S. J., and Stein, B. H. (1980), 'D. C. M. Platt: The anatomy of "autonomy"', *Latin American Research Review*, XV, (1), pp. 131-46.

Sunkel, O. (1977), 'The development of development thinking', in R. Luckham (ed.), 'Imperialism: new tactics', *IDS Bulletin* (Sussex: Institute of Development Studies), 8, (3), March, pp. 6-11.

Suppe, F. (ed.) (1977), *The Structure of Scientific Theories*, 2nd edition (Urbana, Ill.: University of Illinois Press).

Sutcliffe, B. (1972), 'Conclusion' in R. Owen and B. Sutcliffe (eds), *Studies in the Theory of Imperialism* (London: Longman), pp. 312-30.

Tabari, A. (1975), Review of Freedom and development by Julius K. Nyrere, in *Review of African Political Economy*, no. 3, May-September, pp. 89-96.

Taylor, J. G. (1979), *From Modernization to Modes of Production: A Critique of the Sociologies of Development and Underdevelopment* (London: Macmillan).

Tipps, D. (1973), 'Modernization theory and the comparative study of societies: a critical perspective', *Comparative Studies of Society and History*, 15, (2), pp. 199-226.

Toye, J. (1987), *Dilemmas of Development: Reflections on the Counter-Revolution in Development Theory and Policy* (Oxford: Blackwell).

United Nations (1964), *The Economic Development of Latin America in the Post-War Period* (New York: United Nations).

Van Allen, J. (1976), 'African women, "modernization", and national liberation', in L. B. Iglitzin and R. Ross (eds), *Women in the World: A Comparative Study* (Santa Barbara, Ca.: Clio Books), pp. 25-54.

Wade, R., and White, G. (eds) (1984), 'Development states in East Asia: capitalist and socialist', *IDS Bulletin*, 15, (2), April.

Wallerstein, I. (1979), *The Capitalist World Economy* (Cambridge: Cambridge University Press).

Warren, B. (1973), 'Imperialism and capitalist industrialization', *New Left Review*, no. 81, September–October, pp. 3-44.

Warren, B. (1980), *Imperialism: Pioneer of Capitalism* (London: Verso).

Weber, M. (1930), *The Protestant Ethic and the Spirit of Capitalism* (London: Allen & Unwin).

Weber, M. (1948), *From Max Weber: Essays in Sociology*, edited by H. H. Gerth and C. Wright Mills (London: Routledge & Kegan Paul).

Weber, M. (1949), *The Methodology of the Social Sciences* (New York: Free Press).

Weiner, M. (ed) (1966), *Modernization: The Dynamics of Growth* (New York: Basic Books).

White, L. A. (1945), '"Diffusion vs. evolution": an anti-evolutionist fallacy', *American Anthropologist*, 47, (3), July-September, pp. 339-56.

Williams, E. (1964), *Capitalism and Slavery* (London: Deutsch).

Williams, G. (1985), 'Marketing boards in Nigeria', *Review of African Political Economy*, no. 34, December, pp. 4-15.

Wolpe, H. (ed.) (1980), *The Articulation of Modes of Production: Essays from Economy and Society* (London: Routledge & Kegan Paul).

Worsley, P. (1984), *The Three Worlds: Culture and World Development* (London: Weidenfeld & Nicolson).

Young, K., Wolkowitz, C., and McCullagh, R. (eds) (1981), *Of Marriage and the Market: Women's Subordination in International Perspective* (London: CSE Books).

# *Index*